FRAMING THE DEBATE

FRAMING
THE
DEBATE

Famous Presidential Speeches
and How Progressives Can Use
Them to Change the Conversation
(and Win Elections)

JEFFREY FELDMAN
WITH AN INTRODUCTION BY GEORGE LAKOFF

Brooklyn, New York

Printed in Canada
First Paperback Edition
10 9 8 7 6 5 4 3 2 1

Please direct inquiries to:

Ig Publishing
178 Clinton Avenue
Brooklyn, NY 11205
www.igpub.com

Library of Congress Cataloging-in-Publication Data

Feldman, Jeffrey.
  Framing the debate : famous presidential speeches and how progressives can use
them to change the conversation (and win elections) / Jeffrey Feldman.
     p. cm.
  Includes bibliographical references.
  ISBN-13: 978-0-9771972-9-3
  ISBN-10: 0-9771972-9-8
  1. Politics, Practical--United States. 2. Progressivism (United States politics)
3. Presidents--United States--Messages. 4. Communication in politics--
United States.
  I. Title.
  JK1726.F45 2006
  352.23'80973--dc22
                                    2006103349

To my wife Debora

CONTENTS

ACKNOWLEDGMENTS

The daily life of framing relies on the efforts of many more people than could ever be recognized with one pass of the pen. Similarly, this book began as a series of conversations, but then grew into a project that involved more people than I can remember.

I will be forever grateful to Robert Lasner and Elizabeth Clementson of Ig Publishing for their patience and encouragement—particularly for their patience—at every stage of the project.

Presidential speeches are in the public domain, but several electronic resources proved instrumental to this book. I extend a special gratitude to the Scripps Library and Multimedia Archive, which is part of the Miller Center for Public Affairs at the University of Virginia, and to the Speech Archive of the Program in Presidential Rhetoric, part of the Communications Department at Texas A & M University.

I have been fortunate enough to have benefited from the work and encouragement of George Lakoff. Professor Lakoff has been a role model in building a bridge between academia and progressive politics. I am indebted to his work and to the work of the Rockridge Institute.

Framing the Debate first took shape on my "Frameshop" blog diaries at *Daily Kos*, a writing experience that inspired me to start my own weblog. I am incredibly grateful to Markos Moulitsas Zúniga for providing the kind of open forum that encourages progressives to make their voice heard in conversation about America's future. To everyone who has read, commented, encouraged and, when necessary, lambasted my framing advice and warnings in the comment threads on *Daily Kos*: I am indebted to you for your creativity and infectious dedication to driving the debate.

While writing this book, I have enjoyed the opportunity to frame the debate in a variety of venues through the progressive media. I am grateful to Mark Karlin for the opportunity to share my approach to framing and the *Frameshop* website to the readers of *BuzzFlash*. And I extend a special thanks to the *Peter B. Collins Show* and the *Thom Hartmann Radio Program* for inviting me to frame the debate on the growing stage of progressive talk radio.

Each day this book was being written, I have been joined by framers from all over the world who come to the *Frameshop* website because they share a common goal: building a progressive future. This book is dedicated to everyone who helped turn *Frameshop* into a place to shape the debate since I first declared "Frameshop *is* open!"

My family has stood by me from the days that *Frameshop* first took shape and throughout the writing of this book, and I am grateful for their constant encouragement. Above all else, I could not frame, write or think about the future without the support of my wife, Debora. Her humor, trust and love helped shape every page of this book.

INTRODUCTION: FRAMING IS ABOUT IDEAS, AND IDEAS MATTER

By **George Lakoff**

When Barry Goldwater lost the presidential election in 1964, American political debate was framed in liberal terms and few people thought like conservatives. That has changed.

For nearly four decades, conservatives have been framing American political discourse their way, not just in terms of language, but more importantly in terms of their moral system, their values, and their ideas. Over that period, they have spent around four billion dollars on their idea factories—their think tanks—and their message machine: radio and television stations, newspapers and magazines, training institutes, booking agencies, bloggers, ad agencies, and professional crafters of language. The result is that conservative values and ideas have become widespread through America.

Despite the Democratic congressional victories of 2006, those values and ideas are not going to go away. The need for progressives to frame political dialogue in America is every bit as needed now as before the 2006 election.

Frames are mental structures that characterize ideas. Since we think with our brains, any new idea that we learn to think in terms of is represented physically in our brains. For most of the past forty years, conservatives have had a clear field, as progressives did little or nothing to counter the ongoing conservative framing of issues. That began to turn around in 2004, with the work of the Rockridge Institute and the publication of *Don't Think of an Elephant!* and has continued with the publication of *Thinking Points*, Rockridge's handbook for progressives. Progressives throughout America have begun the reframing process and it showed in the 2006 election.

Jeffrey Feldman, writing on his *Frameshop* blog, has been an important voice in the resurgence of progressive framing, and *Framing the Debate* is a significant contribution.

What Feldman has accomplished is a reuniting of contemporary progressive framing efforts with the progressive ideas that have always been at the heart of American democracy. By looking at the framing in presidential speeches, from Washington and Lincoln to Kennedy and Clinton, Feldman reminds us of the central progressive themes in American democracy: Washington's call to service; Lincoln's government of, by and for the people; Franklin Roosevelt's idea that the wealth of this country is in people, not money.

Though this book is pitched as a guide to political rhetoric, it accomplishes a lot more. Feldman explains the difference between a frame and a message. Framing is about one's moral worldview, core values, and underlying principles. Such "deep frames" are largely unconscious and all too often unspoken in progressive discourse. But they are what politics is fundamentally about. Messages, to be successful, depend on deep framing, but are specific communications— say, about particular policies or programs or events.

Political framing is therefore about the big picture, about values and principles. If they are communicated, the surface messages are easier to get across. Moreover, values and principles underlie policies and programs, which is why an understanding of framing is necessary for policy-makers.

Feldman also points out the difference between framing and spin. Spin is the untruthful use of language to get out of an embarrassing situation. Framing, on the other hand, is dedicated to morality and truth: to communicating your values and principles and to framing facts as having a moral value and, often, an ethical imperative.

This book, therefore, provides a corrective to progressives who have fallen into the trap of just stating the facts—as if everyone will thereby reason to the right conclusions without any value-based framing. That rarely happens. Facts don't speak for themselves; facts need value-based frames to become moral imperatives.

This book also serves as a guide to the basics of framing: never use the other side's frames because they carry the other side's values with them. Since words are defined relative to frames, the other side's words will evoke their frames and hence their values. To use their words is to be trapped in their frames.

Feldman is not just writing for candidates and speechwriters. He is writing for all progressives, especially ordinary citizens who want to speak their mind. It is not just presidents who need to think in terms of grand themes; we all do, because those grand themes are what define us as political beings and as having political identities.

What does it mean to be a progressive? The fundamental values are empathy and responsibility to act on that empathy—responsibility both for yourself and for others. From these values, others follow: community and self-government that is both protective and enabling. Protective self-government includes not just the police and the military, but also consumer protection, worker protection, environmental protection, and safety nets. Enabling self-government requires freedom, fairness, opportunity, and shared prosperity. The process of self-government requires the use of common wealth to provide infrastructure, plus political equality, maximal participation, and cooperation, which requires trust, which requires honesty, openness, and accountability.

These are traditional American values, and they lead to traditional American moral and political ideas:

- Empathy leads to a focus on others as well as oneself, and to the idea that causation is systemic and complex, as well as direct.
- Responsibility—moral, legal, and financial—is both individual and social.
- Character is having empathy and acting responsibly on that empathy.
- Moral action is both socially and individually based.
- The role of government is to maximize freedom, both freedom *from* harm and freedom *to* pursue happiness; that is, to be both protector and enabler.
- As protector and enabler for all citizens, government requires the use of the common wealth (taxes) to provide the needed infrastructure for both individuals and businesses: police, the military, disaster protection and relief, and systems that permit transportation, communication, banking, courts, fair and honest markets, fair and honest elections, protection of the environment and public property, education, maximization of health, availability of housing, and so on.
- Moral functions in society require public accountability and, therefore, government regulation and access to the courts. Privatization and deregulation shift governance from the accountable public sphere to the unaccountable private sphere. Privatization and deregulation of services should be avoided when moral functions are at stake, e.g., food safety, drug safety, environmental protection, honest banking, and so on.
- War is inherently destructive and should be avoided unless absolutely necessary for the protection of the population.
- Moral action involves empathy and responsible action in response to that empathy.

These progressive views cannot be taken for granted. For the past four decades, conservatives have been framing public debate in terms of very different ideas.

The heart of conservative thought is the idea of moral authority: that there is an absolute division between good and evil in the world. It is both natural and right that authority should rest with those who are good. Their job is to impose a moral order, in which moral action is obedient to the moral authority, and in which disobedience must be punished to maintain a moral order. Individual discipline is required for moral action. If you obey legal authorities and know right from wrong, the social order should allow you to become your own moral authority in personal spheres of life.

In economic issues, it is assumed that it is natural for people to seek to maximize their self interest and that it is a law of nature that if everyone pursues their own profit, the profit of all will be maximized. The free market is thus moral in that it helps everyone. The free market thus plays the role of the moral authority. Individual discipline is rewarded by the market and the lack of it is punished. Government can only interfere with this natural and moral process.

America is seen as inherently good, and so its interests naturally serve good in the world. This makes America a moral authority in the world. Here are some of the conservative ideas that follow:

- All responsibility—moral, legal, or financial—is individual responsibility.
- Character is moral strength—backbone, discipline, steadfastness.
- Everyone can act morally; all you need is discipline.
- The laissez-faire free market is both natural and moral, and its results are fair.
- Anyone can succeed in a free market; all you need is discipline, that is, character.
- The rich thus deserve their wealth and the poor, their poverty.

- Nature is a resource for human use; it should be turned to profit and property.
- Individual property rights outweigh any common good.
- Government that seeks to help people actually harms people: by giving them things they haven't earned, it takes away their discipline. Such government is bureaucratic, inhuman, oppressive, inefficient, and wasteful.
- Taxes are money that government takes out of the pockets of hard-working citizens and then wastes.
- Private enterprise always performs better than government and should supplant government wherever possible.
- There is an absolute, clearly delineated good and evil, that America is inherently good.
- War in the name of American interests is noble.
- Morality is obedience to a moral authority, and a failure to obey moral authority deserves punishment.

These are among the "conservative" ideas at odds with the progressive moral worldview on which American democracy is based.

Barack Obama, in *The Audacity of Hope*, draws a distinction between ideology and values, as he understands them. "Values are faithfully applied to the facts before us, while ideology overrides whatever facts call theory into question." If we apply the Obama criterion to the two moral worldviews given above, the question becomes: Which ideas about government actually help and which actually harm?

The progressive argument is that progressive ideas about government actually help people and conservative ideas actually harm them. The Iraq War harmed people, both Americans and Iraqis. Conservative policies that downgraded FEMA and redirected funds for levee repair to tax breaks hurt people affected by Hurricane Katrina. Education policies have hurt the public schools and students needing college loans. Conservative environmental policies have been disastrous for the environment. Conservative housing policies have increased homelessness. Conservative health policies have left 46 million people without health care. And on and on.

Raising the minimum wage would help people. Universal health care would help people. Preserving the environment and addressing global warming would help people. Serious disaster relief would help people. Real post-Katrina reconstruction efforts would help people.

By the Obama criterion, the progressive worldview counts as "values" and the conservative worldview as "ideology." In short, they are not simply different but equal opinions. They are ideas that matter to people.

That is why it is vital for progressives to learn to frame political discourse. Framing is about ideas and values. Ideas and values matter. A lot.

PREFACE

"Progressive is a complex word because it depends on the significantly complicated history of the word progress."
—(Raymond Williams, *Keywords*)[1]

The term "progressive" is new enough to the contemporary political scene that, if asked to define it, an equal number of Americans are as likely to think "auto insurance" as "political paradigm." And yet, "progressive" as a word used to describe an approach to American politics is at least a century old.

In the first half of the twentieth century, the U.S. political system witnessed the birth of three different progressive parties—the first founded by Theodore Roosevelt in 1912, a second founded by Robert Marion La Follette, Sr. in 1924, and a third founded by Franklin Roosevelt's former Vice President, Henry Wallace in 1948.[2] As it happens, progressive is not a new political term at all, but a time honored word with a distinguished history that has been miraculously, albeit not immaculately, reborn.

Since the Presidential election of 2004, a huge effort has been underfoot in America to define and understand a new progressive movement with the specific goal of restoring all that has been abused, dismantled and destroyed by six years of rule by an unchecked Republican Party. That effort was emboldened by the 2006 election victories that swept Democrats to the majority status in Congress, making the hope of building a progressive future in America feel like a true possibility. The concept of "framing" has played a central role in all these efforts.

While the ultimate goal of progressive framing since 2004 has been to help the Democratic Party win elections, the strategy has also involved two critical developments unheard of in recent times. The first is a massive push by ordinary citizens into the day-to-day processes of electoral politics. Unlike past Democratic Party efforts at "outreach," this new phenomenon can be described as a "reaching up" by hitherto uninvolved citizens driven to new levels of political involvement by virtue of a concern for the future of the country.

Building on this new involvement, the second development has been a wide scale effort to identify and understand the principles of the Democratic Party, and to find the best way to communicate them persuasively to the American people. In this context, many new arrivals to the fold of Democratic Party politics see "framing the debate" not only as fundamental political work, but as a defining aspect of the progressive movement and as such, indispensable to the long-term goal of restoring fairness, responsibility and honesty to American government.

Two-hundred years from now, historians may refer to the progressive movement of early twenty-first century American politics as the "laptop revolution"—the emergence of a politics driven by blogs, media and internet communication. But the remarkable transformation unfolding in American politics under the rubric of "progressivism" is much more significant than any single form of technology or any particular aspect of the rapidly changing world of global media. What is truly new in this time period is the emergence of a completely novel form of political activism—a form of political engagement previously reserved only for the backroom of political consultants. What are truly new are the framers.

Some framers are bloggers, some are organizers, some are activists, but they are all progressive Americans interested in and concerned about the future. Each day, tens of thousands of these framers, most of whom see themselves as progressive members of the Democratic Party, awake with the goal of framing the debate. Each day, these framers track down and read news stories and political speeches in order to understand the implications of their cognitive and narrative logic. And each day, they send their analysis through the myriad open doors feeding back into the media. Armed only with an internet connection, a rough understanding of linguistics, and their unshakable beliefs, these framers are convinced they can beat back the hourly onslaught of propaganda flooding America. And they can.

The idea that a principled citizenry should take up the task of monitoring and speaking back to its government is as old as the United States Constitution itself, but the drive to do it each and every day by framing the debate is new—a product of the sheer quantity of work required to hold the line in defense of democracy during the presidency of George W. Bush. And beyond the daily work of framing, progressives have also begun the important work of rooting their day-to-day efforts in the long tradition of American words and ideas.

Framing the Debate is both a guide to those framers who have begun the work, and an invitation to a new generation of progressive framers who are just now making the decision to take up framing. Due to the busy nature of our lives and the urgency of contemporary politics, it is impossible for all of us on our own to delve into the American tradition of framing political ideas. *Framing the Debate*, therefore, brings together fifteen great examples from the history of Presidential speeches, analyzes them using the "framing tools" that I have developed through my *Frameshop* website over the past two years, and then applies key lessons to the current debate.

Now more than ever, the success of progressive framers depends on the ability to keep one's head safely above the rising waters of spin, particularly in the intense moments leading up to hotly contested, media driven elections. With those moments in mind, *Framing the Debate* has been written for progressives seeking new tools to help repair political debate, today, and to help build a progressive vision for the long road ahead.

Jeffrey Feldman
New York City
December 2006

1. FRAMERS AND FRAMING

A routine search for the word "framer" in the *American Heritage Dictionary* brings back the following peculiar definition:

> NOUN: 1. One that frames: *a picture framer; a framer of new laws*. 2. often **Framer**: One of the people who wrote the U.S. Constitution.[1]

What an astounding range of possibilities! One the one hand, a "framer" is a person engaged in the simple act of packaging pictures, while on the other hand a "Framer"—with a capital "F"—is a founder, one of the people who thought up and crafted the principles that shape the entire American system of government. From the mundane to the profound and back again—the concept of "framing" covers it all.

What we see from the definition, however, is that in the context of American history, there are few concepts more important and enduring than framing. This country began with an act of framing, and to this day continues to forge ahead—sometimes for better, sometimes for worse—through quiet, but powerful framing.

And yet, despite its historic footing, many people often react to the idea of framing political debate with suspicion, concerned that framers engage in little more than the cynical packaging of ideas for political gain. "It's the substance that matters, not the wrapper," they say. In fact, framing the debate is never just about the wrapper. To make rotten politics smell better by wrapping them in clean paper is the goal of "spin," or deception, not of framing. Indeed, we should be opposed to the increasing number of "spin doctors" who use their skill at mass manipulation to pollute American politics. Unfortunately, as long as there are scandals in politics, there will be spin doctors to make the smell seem less offensive. While both framing and spin involve the packaging of ideas, "framing the debate" is as different from spin as coffee is to whiskey.

What Does "Framing the Debate" Mean?

A basic working definition of "framing" as it pertains to political debate looks something like this:

> The presentation of political ideas and principles so as to encourage one interpretation over another.

But in a much broader sense, beyond politics, framing has long been in use across a variety of professions and academic disciplines interested in how people communicate with each other, experience the world around them, and solve their problems.

In the 1950's, for example, anthropologist Gregory Bateson likened frames to the body, focusing, through studies of children at play, on how bodily gestures and facial expressions framed communicative interaction.[2] Similarly, in the 1960s, sociologist Erving Goffman considered the full range of human behavior as a series of framed interactions, where one social actor uses words, phrases, or gestures to communicate what kind of social interaction was appropriate in a given moment.[3] A decade later, linguists Richard Bandler and John Grinder modeled individual speech habits to help reframe people's unconscious towards therapeutic ends.[4] In the 1990s, business and legal scholars in the Harvard Negotiation Project, such as Douglas Stone, considered how conversations could be approached so as to mitigate blame and lead to productive outcomes.[5] In each of these fields, "frame" and "framing" had a slightly different meaning, but always referred to a broad logic or context through which key events unfolded. And in each case, the scholar would compare a frame to something else to help explain what exactly was meant by "framing."

Despite the fascinating aspects of each of these other approaches, framing did not enter progressive politics with full force until cognitive linguist George Lakoff published his book *Don't Think of An Elephant!* just prior to the 2004 presidential election.[6] Different from all other approaches to framing, Lakoff began by considering a very basic and very grounded question:

Why do Democrats lose elections?

Because Lakoff's book coincided with President George W. Bush's stunning—to progressives—re-election against the Democratic nominee, Senator John Kerry, this initial question quickly morphed into a more chilling and timely inquiry:

Why did Bush win again?

Up to this point, most progressives had assumed that Kerry was a better candidate. Setting aside all dirty campaigning from the nefarious allies of Bush, Kerry seemed to present key positions and issues that were more relevant to the problems Americans faced than those presented by Bush. Kerry was more thoughtful and informed than Bush. The conventional progressive wisdom was that Kerry should have won the election.

But with Lakoff's question in mind and a bit of hindsight, most progressives now realize that something was amiss in our understanding of the 2004 election. Looking back, we realize that the debates between Kerry and Bush were a key point in the campaign, albeit for a reason that was unexpected at the time. While Kerry clearly gave the better performance, he failed to gain what many expected to be a considerable bounce in the polls. It was a desperate feeling for many idealistic progressives who believed that Kerry had the right ideas and was so much more articulate than Bush. Kerry might have seemed a bit stiff, but he certainly was smart, prepared, and statesman-like. He was even taller. Bush, by contrast, was cocky, he stuttered, endlessly repeated the same words, and even balked on many answers. He was even caught wearing a wire that many believed was used to feed him answers by closed circuit radio!

I remember the questions I asked myself in that week following the debates when I realized that the polls had not shifted definitively as a result of the two candidates' debate performances. "Aren't we supposed to win when we present the best ideas in the clearest way? Aren't we supposed to win when their candidate acts and looks unprepared and uniformed? Aren't we supposed to win when the majority of the electorate agrees with what our guy is saying?"

Interestingly, the dynamic my questions identified fit right in with what Lakoff was talking about. The problem was not the positions and issues the Democratic candidate presented, but how Democrats approached the entire idea of political debate. My candidate might have won the debates on the issues, but he lost the larger battle of the election because the opposition controlled the frame—and therefore framed the debate. We were talking issues, but they were invoking frames.

From Lakoff's perspective frames are defined as:

> mental structures that shape the way we see the world . . .
> You can't see or hear frames . . . When you hear a word, its
> frame is activated in your brain.[7]

Intellectually, Lakoff's definition put forward the general perspective of a cognitive linguist who views speech and communication as a product of certain big ideas and concepts that have been hardwired into our brains through habit and experience. He then applied those concepts to the specifics of American politics over the past thirty years. Even without delving into the technical workings of the brain, this insight opened a profound discussion of why and how the Republicans won in 2004, and engendered a new, eye-opening perspective on political debate for progressives.

Whereas progressives had previously understood political debate as a forum for presenting policy and issues, framing redefined political debate as a stage for invoking principles and values through keywords, metaphors, and strategic phrases. Winning the debate—and by extension winning elections—would be the result of driving the debate towards progressive frames and, most importantly, keeping it there.

While progressive ideas may have been good, we lost elections because the opposition chose words that invoked powerful sets of unspoken ideas that structured the entire debate. These ideas described a worldview of how the country should work that ultimately trumped and undermined every possible statement made by progressive candidates. While Democrats were obsessing over the best words to use in order to give people the facts, the Republicans chose words that repackaged the conceptual framework through which the entire American public saw the world. Those Republican "magic words" were then repeated and amplified endlessly by the media—not just by *FOX News*, but by all media and even by progressive candidates themselves. And so, the Republicans won because their words drove and held the frame.

When progressives take on the task of framing the debate, election campaigns become much broader struggles to establish the vision, principles, and worldview of a candidate. For decades, Republicans have made great strides establishing what they call a "conservative" worldview which consists of strong, authoritarian perspectives about the right of government to intervene in the private lives of citizens, the priority of particular religious values over constitutional principles, divestment from public ownership and the public good, concentration of private wealth, and preemptive military aggression. In many ways, President Bush's victories in 2000 and

2004 were the product of several decades of this relentless framing of the "conservative" worldview.[8]

In the 2006 midterm elections, Democratic framing efforts finally began to get some traction. A broad initiative to frame veterans running for election as "Fighting Dems" helped drive the debate towards a progressive vision of responsible change in the Iraq. While not all "Fighting Dems" managed to eke out victories at the polls, the frame helped to dispel the myth of Democrats being weak on defense. In another framing initiative, the progressive grassroots organization MoveOn.org framed their pre-election voter outreach program through the telephone frame by launching the volunteer initiative "Call For Change." At a technical level, "Call for Change" was not much different from previous volunteer phone bank operations designed to encourage Democrats to vote. However, by framing the often unappealing concept of campaign volunteering through the concrete metaphor of "telephone calls," the MoveOn.org program had unprecedented success, bringing in far more people and contacting far more voters. Such an effort demonstrated once and for all that framing helps to define and extend a progressive worldview in key political moments, which in turn leads to greater participation and deeper commitment to the work needed for campaigns to succeed.

But even with these first Progressive framing successes in 2006, many questions remained. Paramount among them: What is the progressive worldview? Despite the 2006 election success, many progressives still had a lingering sense that they were struggling against conservative frames at least as much as advancing their own unique worldview. And that was no accident. For over twenty years, advocates of the conservative movement had lured progressives into a fight they could not win a fight that left the words "liberal" and "Democrat" bloodied and hanging on the ropes. The endless beating-up of these words by conservative think tanks, broadcast media, and church leaders had convinced many Americans that the Democratic Party was not only incapable of governing, but was an immoral choice at the polls.

After years of bloody losses against conservative efforts, the sudden interest in framing by progressives in late 2004 suggested a radical new tactic, and the progressive successes of 2006 proved that that tactic could work if applied broadly. Rather than try to win the battle of worldviews inside the ring of ideas and political positions crafted by conservative strategists, progressives could walk out of the conservative ring into one of their own. To stop bleeding and start winning, progressives looked beyond defensive, reactionary approaches to political debate and rebuild the debate on progressive terms from the ground up.

And yet, as genuine and explosive as the enthusiasm for framing the debate became amongst progressive leaders, activists and citizens alike, a vexing question appeared on the road to Damascus:

> How can progressives continue to frame the political debate moving forward?

How can framing continue to work in practice? For every book, letter to the editor, seminar and blog post urging progressives to start framing the debate, there were a dozen responses that asked that same basic question: "How?" Now that the 2006 elections have proven that framing the debate is crucial for advancing a progressive vision and winning elections, the question has become: "What do we do next?"

Framing in Five Steps

Becoming a progressive framer begins with changing a set of habits with respect to how we receive and process information. Framers make a choice to stop being passive consumers of political debate and to start producing the debate themselves—to seek out the situations where politics happens and drive the debate. Progressive framers must be willing to step into the shoes of the traditional media. Gone are the days of reading one daily newspaper to get information; framers must read dozens of sources each day, tracking political ideas and issues as they take shape across the broad landscape of media-driven contemporary politics.

Blogs are the central haunting ground for progressive framers because they offer a nexus between political organizations, mass media, and the chatter of popular culture. A remarkable feature of the world we live in today is that most words politicians utter in public are instantly made available to everyone. Every public word President Bush says, for example, appears within minutes on the White House website.[9] Progressive framers must be willing to track down what is broadcast on television, radio and the internet in order to tease out the frames at work in the broader debate and, whenever necessary, reframe the debate in progressive terms.

In addition, progressive framers must never be satisfied to frame the debate only for themselves. Just like the old adage about whether a tree that falls in the woods makes a sound if nobody is there to hear it, when progressives frame the debate on their own, but do not communicate that effort to others, does it have an impact? Clearly, communicating the results of any progressive effort to frame the debate has a wider impact than keeping that effort hidden from others. And once the choice to communicate has been made, the work of framing can begin immediately.

In November 2004, I made the choice to become a progressive framer by establishing a website called *Frameshop* (www.frameshopisopen.com), a place for communicating the results of my work throughout the progressive movement. At the outset, I defined *Frameshop* as more than a website, more than a blog. It was and continues to be a "place" for framing the debate.

Frameshop is not just a clearing house for my opinions. It's a "repair shop." It's a noisy, dirty place. There's grease on our policy coveralls. Broken sound bite pieces are lying around in open bins. Protective eyewear is required at all times. I begin with the idea that political debate in this country is a highway filled with language long due for repairs. During election time, political debate becomes a racetrack. Even the fastest phrases will crash and burn after a few laps if not properly maintained. In debate, like in driving: paint looks pretty, but it's what's under the hood that matters.

Frameshop began with this basic metaphor about "driving" and "repairing" the debate. Yet, over the course of hundreds of "repair jobs"— long and short essays in which I reframed key aspects of the political debate—a five-step approach to framing the debate took shape. [10]

Step One: Stop Repeating their Words

When the opposition controls the debate by setting the frame, the only way out is to stop using the language provided by the opposition. Repetition is how a frame is reinforced, so the only way to break it is to stop repeating the words that evoke it. This may seem artificial at first, but without this first step, it will not be possible to take control of the debate. Remember that a well-set frame allows plenty of latitude for an opposing point of view.

Step Two: Go to Another Frame

For most people, this will be the hardest concept to understand. "Wait a minute! There are other frames out there for me to go to? You make frames sound like rooms in a house." In fact, frames are not quite rooms, but it can be helpful to think of a frame metaphorically as a place rather than a set of ideas. One of the best ways to go to another frame is to immerse oneself in the political speech of another time period in American politics. To go to another frame when reading about healthcare for example, one might read a speech by Franklin Roosevelt. To go to another frame when debating national security, one might read a speech by Woodrow Wilson. To go to another frame when thinking about participation in government, one might read a speech by John Kennedy.

Step Three: Build a New Frame

Now the work of building up a new frame begins. First, ask what principle this particular issue is all about. For example, in a discussion of Social Security, Republicans claim the issue is "personal wealth."

Progressives, by contrast, believe the debate is about the value of "protection" and the principle of "investment in the public good." Here, to frame the debate, we can tell a story about the role Social Security as an investment that protects the public, and create new phrases based on a central metaphor for Social Security. In general, a metaphor in politics takes the form of two concepts brought into the same idea:

[abstract issue] is [a concrete thing][11]

The result is that we understand one in terms of the other—the abstract issue in terms of the concrete thing and vice versa. For example, Republicans base their talking points about Social Security in terms of this metaphor:

[Social Security] is [a bank account]

And all their fancy magic words (e.g., "personal retirement accounts") follow from that metaphor. A progressive frame for Social Security, by contrast, might begin with a different metaphor:

[Social Security] is [a person]

This metaphor can provide the broad logic for progressives to generate new statements about Social Security "standing by those in need" and "extending a hand." By reframing Social Security in this way, it ceases to be about writing checks to seniors, but becomes about protection and the public good. It is the hand of the nation reaching out to older workers to guide them safely out of the work force, while at the same time making room for younger workers. Thus, a new frame begins to take shape.[12]

Step Four: Break It Down
A frame is a big narrative painted in broad strokes. Thus far, it is a narrative about principles, people and government. To make a frame

ready for use on websites, speeches, ads, letters, platforms, fundraisers, and debates, we first need to break it down into bite-sized pieces. Breaking it down requires a great deal of brainstorming and trial-and-error before the best phrases emerge.

Step Five: Repeat Our Words

Repetition—the very thing we stopped when we began this process—is where we return to set up the new frame we have created. Once we eliminate the use of conservative keywords, we now craft our own messages that make use of those words and phrases that evoke the progressive principles and logic of our new frame.

Framing Is Action

Beyond the question of "how" to turn broad theory into the actual day-to-day process of framing the debate, a second—and often much more barbed—question inevitably emerges:

Aren't actions more important than words?

The question about framing the debate not being about actual political action is often accompanied by angry refrains of "Stop trying to manipulate people!" and "Just say what you mean!" or "I'm tired of framing! Get out there and do something already!"

Whether or not framing the debate will be a form of political action palatable to every progressive depends on the priorities and personality of each person. Progressive politics is a large project and not everyone will be involved in the same daily activities. A division of labor is important in any grand venture. But make no mistake about it, framing is action.

Over more than two centuries, our population has grown and scattered across the nation. While our political system was established at a time when most people never traveled more than one hundred miles away from their homes during their entire lives, today most of us travel that far each week. In recent decades Americans have found new ways to traverse that expanse and reconnect to each other with startling efficiency and regularity. Framing the debate is political action because, now more than ever, American politics takes place in a vast electronic town square where the price of admission is a laptop computer and political action is a non-stop conversation unfolding in words and images.

One way to register how quickly politics has changed is to consider the difference between the political scandals of today and the political scandals of previous generations. The Republican Watergate scandal, for example, began with a late-night burglary. The story then unfolded piece by piece over many months of investigations by two reporters at one print newspaper, *The Washington Post*.

Fast-forward thirty years. The Republican "Foleygate" scandal began with an inappropriate email, then exploded in a matter of hours due to millions of ordinary citizens' investigations and conversations across blogs, instant messages, and email. At one time, Americans waited for political debate to arrive in the morning paper or with the flip of a television "on" switch; just one generation later, individual, but technologically connected, citizens are the engine that drives the political debate. The day has finally come when "We the People" is more than just "We the Media," as journalist Dan Gilmore suggests.[13] "We"—what we do and we say—has become political debate itself.

In this new reality in which we find ourselves, framing the debate will always be different than running for public office, walking door-to-door to register new voters, or working as a polling volunteer on election night. But framing the debate is no less "real" a form of political action.

American Roots

In laying out "Framing in Five Steps," I suggested that reading the speeches of past progressives can help framers to think their way out of whatever language might dominate a current issue. Reading a speech with those five steps in mind is a way of rising above the often-deafening political buzz of the current debate, and is an important tactic for framers to use. But beyond just treating past speeches as temporary narrative safe havens, progressive framers must also develop the habit and practice of reading American political speeches for another reason: to grow roots.

Having applied lessons in cognitive and narrative science to framing political debate, the crucial next step for progressives is to ground their framing efforts in the tradition of American political speech. Rooting contemporary efforts at framing the debate in the long heritage of American efforts at framing is not just a good idea, but the critical second half of the progressive framing puzzle. To be truly effective, progressive framers must build a bridge between the contemporary need to advance a progressive vision—to win elections—and the long history of progressive ideas that echo up from America's political past. Without building that bridge between past and present American voices, progressive frames risk crafting a political debate that—while effective in scientific principle—is culturally rootless.

Framing, as we recall from the definition that opened this chapter, is most widely understood by Americans as the work that produced the core document of progressive politics: the Constitution of the United States. To succeed, current progressive framing must connect to the long road of ideas the stretches from the framers of the Constitution, through each period in American history, into the new cultural and political challenges of today.

While many progressive framers will be familiar with one or two great American political speeches, most have yet to consider them with the toolkit and mandate of framing. Seen through the eyes of a framer thinking about the best way to drive the contemporary debate towards a progressive vision, past political speeches become a vast, untapped landscape of ideas and resources for the task of framing.

One particular genre of American political speech is particularly rich in possibilities for contemporary progressives: presidential speeches. By virtue of their cultural prominence and wide circulation, presidential speeches are a familiar form of public speech. In particular, the great Presidential speeches—those words that have been played and replayed so many times that they have achieved iconic status in the American imagination—provide windows onto key approaches to framing that are applicable to present day circumstances.

While past Presidents addressed the entire country in these speeches, the task of progressive framers is to find lessons for three groups central to progressive politics:

- **Politicians**—Elected officials and candidates
- **Activists**—Campaign workers and organizers
- **Citizens**—Individual voters

For each act of reconnaissance and analysis into a past presidential speech, the task at hand for contemporary framers is to find key framing lessons that can be directly applied to the concerns and needs of these three categories of progressives. Thus, progressive framers become much more than readers of classic speeches—they become mediators of contemporary progressive politics and the American tradition of political ideas.

One caveat, however, is absolutely critical for any progressive who makes the important choice to take on the responsibility of bridging past and present: key lessons in progressive framing are not determined by the party affiliation of the speaker. In fact, a crucial oversight often committed by progressives—an error that springs from idealism, not malice—is to see progressive framing lessons only in the speeches of presidents or politicians who self-identified as progressives. In fact, the lessons are everywhere. Once the Pandora's box of presidential speeches is opened, progressive framers will find lessons and resources in every corner.

Hence, in the analysis of presidential speeches that follow in the chapters ahead, an inaugural address by Franklin Roosevelt provides several key framing lessons for progressives, as does the resignation speech of Richard Nixon. The inaugural address of Thomas Jefferson holds important framing lessons for progressives, as does the farewell address of Ronald Reagan. Not just Bill Clinton, but also Dwight Eisenhower. Not just Teddy Roosevelt, but also George W. Bush.

How To Use This Book

Each chapter of *Framing the Debate* begins with a list of keywords and strategies that will emerge from the discussion of the specific presidential speech, followed by an extended quote from the speech itself. The section that follows is a general analysis of the framing techniques and lessons in the speech as a whole. These lessons are then applied to sample "real world" situations relevant to the needs of the "politician," "activist," and individual "citizen." Each applied lesson includes not only a description of the problem at hand, but suggested phrases and messages that can be used.

To be successful, however, framers must do more than lift a set of phrases from a book and paste it into a political campaign: they must craft the best message to suit their framing needs based on the reality on the ground. As such, the suggestions in the chapters ahead are meant as openers—starting points for framing specific debates. Of course, activists seeking to frame the debate might not find the most relevant suggestions in the sections labeled "activist." They might find more apt discussions in those sections sketched out for politicians. Likewise, politicians might find the advice most applicable to their needs in the sections addressed to "citizens." This overlap is very much an intended part of the design of this book. While the framing suggestions in the pages that follow run in chronological order from the oldest presidential speeches to the newest—from George Washington to George W. Bush—they are intended to function not as a list, but as conversation. *Framing the Debate*, in this respect, is as much a reference book and tool kit as it is a linear introduction to presidential speeches and framing.

Ultimately, once progressive framers delve into the resource of presidential speeches, the rest of American political rhetoric opens up as well. Presidential speeches, by virtue of their familiarity and their availability, are an ideal starting point for progressive framers. But the roots of progressive framing extend far beyond the Commander-in-Chief to the full range of great speeches in our country's past, including speeches by civil rights leaders, labor leaders, and military leaders—too name just a few. The American roots of progressive framing can, and should, run as deep and wide as our curiosity. The speeches in *Framing the Debate* serve as an important starting point, but there are many more great examples to be mined. Thus, progressive framing becomes a much broader project than the pragmatics of winning elections suggests. With roots deep in the American tradition of great speeches, progressive framing becomes essential to building bridges between those instances of framing on which the United States was founded and the ongoing efforts at framing that drives the country towards a more progressive future.

Our work has just begun.

2. VOICE OF THE COUNTRY

GEORGE WASHINGTON, *FIRST INAUGURAL ADDRESS* (1789)[1]

Keywords: calling, country, humble, obedience, servant, voice

Strategy: Guest Star Citizens—Tell Your Story—No Pay

Quote

"Among the vicissitudes incident to life, no event could have filled me with greater anxieties than that of which the notification was transmitted by your order, and received on the fourteenth day of the present month. On the one hand, I was summoned by my Country, whose voice I can never hear but with veneration and love, from a retreat which I had chosen with the fondest predilection, and, in my flattering hopes, with an immutable decision, as the asylum of my declining years: a retreat which was rendered every day more necessary as well as more dear to me, by the addition of habit to inclination, and of frequent interruptions in my health to the gradual waste committed on it by time. On the other hand, the magnitude and difficulty of the trust to which the voice of my Country called me, being sufficient to awaken in the wisest and most experienced of her citizens, a distrustful scrutiny into his qualification, could not but overwhelm with despondence, one, who, inheriting inferior endowments from nature and unpracticed in the duties of civil administration, ought to be peculiarly conscious of his own deficiencies. In this conflict of emotions, all I dare aver, is, that it has been my faithful study to collect my duty from a just appreciation of every circumstance, by which it might be affected. All I dare hope, is, that, if in executing this task I have been too much swayed by a grateful remembrance of former instances, or by an affectionate sensibility to this transcendent proof, of the confidence of my fellow-citizens; and have thence too little consulted my incapacity as well as disinclination for the weighty and untried cares before me; my error will be palliated by the motives which misled me, and its consequences be judged by my Country, with some share of the partiality in which they originated."

ANALYSIS

On first glance, one might look at the opening lines of George Washington's first inaugural address and be inclined to prescribe the former General some anti-anxiety medication. "No event could have filled me with greater anxieties," the speech began, "than of which the notification was transmitted by your order and received on the fourteenth day of the present month." Just to make sure I have this right: the first President of the United States, so-called "Father" of the nation, leader of the Revolutionary War, soldier, husband, hero, claims in his inaugural speech that he was "filled with . . . anxieties" just because he was notified of his election to the Presidency? Crossing the Potomac in winter, facing down British troops, posing endlessly for a painting that was never finished—if these tense and time-consuming activities had filled Washington with anxiety, that would have made sense. But the Presidency?

Taking a second more studied look at the speech, however, it becomes clear that Washington's feigned anxiety was more rhetoric than nerves. Even if Washington really was anxious that day, he certainly did not plan to include reference to it in his prepared remarks. Rather, what we hear in the speech was Washington's use of eighteenth century prose to evoke the first frame in the first words in the first speech by a U.S. President.

As always, the frame sets in place the broad logic through which the listener understands not just what the President is saying in a speech, but how we are to understand the meaning of his words. Who are we in this speech? How do we relate to the President? What is America? What are my responsibilities? While a speech delivered by a President may not pose or answer each one of these questions separately, the broad conceptual frame of the speech provides an overarching logic that allows us to understand what is being said.

In Washington's speech, the audience was presented with the "humble servant" frame, as Washington depicts himself as a lowly servant called upon by his country to serve the greater good. America, in this instance, is described as a wise, old person, more powerful than the individual, nervous President. Saying that America has a "voice" that "called" him to service is the core metaphor of the "humble servant" frame, which ultimately defines the relationship between President and People along the lines of servant and master. The President, as Washington describes himself, is a humble servant to the vocal master that is his country.

The "humble servant" frame may seem a bit archaic to Americans today, largely because political speeches are no longer written in the grand style we associate with dusty eighteenth-century novels. But in Washington's time, the "humble servant" frame would have been a familiar style of speech, understood by everyone. In particular, as he delivered it that day, Washington's "humble servant" frame would have brought to mind the rhetorical style of one of the most famous books of the time: the Bible. Through their experience with the Bible, Washington's contemporaries would have understood the "humble servant" frame from their knowledge of encounters between God and the various biblical prophets and heroes. In Genesis 22, for example, God tells Abraham to sacrifice his son; Abraham, in turn, humbly obeys the command. In Exodus 3, God calls Moses to lead the Israelite slaves out of Egypt; Moses, in turn, humbly obeys the command. And again in Exodus 20, God calls Moses to bring down the Ten Commandments; and Moses humbly obeys. In each of these Biblical episodes, the lowly individual was humbled and filled with anxiety upon hearing the great voice of a powerful entity, but then obediently answered the call of that great voice.

In Washington's speech, however, the voice that did the calling was not the voice of God, even though God's name was invoked elsewhere in the speech. Instead, Washington claimed the "voice" he heard was that of "my country," a phrase that Washington repeated three times in his opening paragraph alone. His repetitive use of these words early in the speech are the keys to his framing. By talking about the relationship between the citizens of the United States and the new President as if they were father and son—the citizens being the collective father, the President being the son—Washington wanted his audience to know that he understood and believed that he had not been elected King or Emperor, but President—a constitutionally defined office appointed by the people. And even though he was the man being inaugurated, he wanted his audience to know that they ruled over him, not the other way around.

Washington's "humble servant" frame is centered on the recurrent use of words that express the qualities and actions of the "country" in terms that one would more readily associate with a person. A country for example, cannot "call" anyone. But to talk about his "country" as having a "voice" and as commanding respect and "obedience," Washington defined the newly established constitutional nation in venerable terms, instilling it with the attributes of respect, reverence and even wisdom.

What, then, is the use in today's political world for a frame that defines the President as a humble servant answering to the voice of the country? Because citizens today feel more frustrated than at almost any other time in our nation's history that their elected officials do not listen to them, the possibilities are profound for applying Washington's idea to contemporary politics. In the face of this public frustration, the "humble servant" frame is a basic strategy for establishing a deep relationship between the people and the president, offering the sense that a president is listening to, answering to, and otherwise responsible to the people.

The following are a few scenarios where the "humble servant" frame can be an effective way to drive the debate towards progressive ideals.

STRATEGY

[Politician]—Guest Star Citizens

One of the most annoying habits that presidents have picked up over the past twenty-five years is to have a "guest star citizen" present at a major speech. At some point in the speech, the president will raise a point about education or job training or health care or a military operation and emphasize that point by gesturing towards a "guest star citizen" in the audience whose personal story illustrates the issue. This anonymous, typically very uncomfortable person, then stands up as the audience responds dutifully with applause.

This technique is annoying because while the point of the "guest star citizen" is to make the speech more personal, we all know that the President is not really friends with this person. And yet, despite the fact that nobody reacts on an emotional level to this technique anymore (if they ever did), presidents and politicians keep using it.

Washington's inaugural speech suggests a better way to express a personal bond with the American people. To foster a stronger sense of connection with the audience, progressive candidates can use Washington's "humble servant" frame by gesturing to the collective "voice" of the country instead of spotlighting one person. In this respect, we must remember that Washington did not refer to the plural "voices" of his countrymen, but to one singular "voice." Why? Because he wanted to emphasize that he saw himself as an equal to every American and—at the same time—that he believed himself responsible to the nation as a whole. Based on the way Americans speak today, it is probably better to avoid saying my country, using instead the less presumptuous, "*the* country."

For example, in a speech that references Social Security, a progressive candidate might say, "As I face the challenges that lie ahead, I have heard the voice of the country charging me to defend and strengthen Social Security."

[Activist]—Tell Your Story

One thing that progressives often forget to do, both in formal speeches and informal political debate, is to tell other Americans what it's like to be "called" to public service. Washington's speech, with its tale of his receiving the call to be President, reminds us all how much we often overlook telling our own stories.

As progressives, we want to cut immediately to facts: to talk about policy details and tax increase revenues and distinctions between health care plans. Numbers and details are important, but driving the debate towards progressive ideas requires that people know the big story about why our candidates, representatives and voters are progressive in the first place. Telling our story simply means voicing the moment when we first decided to take on the responsibility to help build a progressive future. What situation, or person, had such a big impact on our lives that we heard—really heard—the voice of our country?

Having located that moment in our life, how do we tell the story? The details are ours, but for an idea of how to turn those details into a story, all we need to do is take a look at Washington's speech. His story of being called to the Presidency can be broken down into four basic components that everyone can use to build their own story:

- What were you doing at the time you got "the call?"
- The event or moment that inspired you to service
- How you felt at that moment
- What action did you take immediately after that

To restate Washington's story (in my own words):

- I had just headed off to my retirement, was enjoying myself at home, looking forward to horseback riding . . .
- When suddenly I received notification that I had been elected by the new government to be the first President of the United States.
- I felt pretty nervous at first . . .
- But then I decided to hold off on retirement and accept this historic role.

It's that easy. So, the next time you are at the dinner table with a family member and the discussion turns to tax cuts or foreign policy or Social Security reform, steal a page from George Washington's speech by stepping back from the details of the discussion to tell your story.

[Citizen]—No Pay

The minimum wage is a hot topic in contemporary political debate. Should it be raised? If it is raised, will the increase in pay have a deleterious impact on the economy? Should politicians vote themselves a raise in pay without first raising the pay of working Americans?

Typically, the economics of the minimum wage conversation overwhelm the discussion. In fact, however, the minimum wage conversation is only about money on the level of policy. At the level of progressive principles, the minimum wage is about "fair employment" and "opportunity for all." But how can this subject matter be engaged without being drawn into the "conservative" frame about money and markets?

One solution is to bring up the subject of government service. Midway through Washington's inaugural address, for example, he announced to his audience, "I must decline as inapplicable to myself, any share in the personal emoluments, which may be indispensably included in a permanent provision for the Executive Department." Translation: No pay for me!

Talking about politicians whose dedication to raising the minimum wage has led them to refuse their own salaries frames the debate in terms of fairness. Obviously, the refusal of pay for public service is not possible for everyone, and it was Washington's elite status as a landholder that enabled him to take that step.

But whatever Washington's class and status, the lesson for contemporary progressives is profound. For a public official to stand up and say, "I will not accept pay," is an excellent way to frame the debate in terms of public good over personal gain. While we are taught as children about Washington's honesty—through the story of his having chopped down a cherry tree and then telling the truth about his misdeed—as adults we would be much better served to remember him as the President who stood up and said, "No pay for me!"

One way to bring this subject up is to invoke the "long line" of American politicians who have rejected their pay out of principle:

> Look, many American leaders both past and present have chosen principle over their own salaries. Even George Washington refused his pay as President so as not avoid any conflict. I am not suggesting that Senators, Representatives, and the President should work without pay. But is it **fair** for our elected officials to continue to increase their pay to keep in line with the rising cost of living when they reject that same possibility for millions of working Americans?

Mentioning Washington's rejection of his salary is part of a strategy of framing a debate about the minimum wage in terms of fairness instead of money. But keep in mind that rejection of pay for public service is not the only way to express the frame of "fairness." Pay can also be delayed until a minimum wage bill is passed. Salary can be rejected, but pension accepted. A pay rate commensurate with a more modest salaried profession can be elected instead of the salary stipulated by law. There are many ways to say it, but the message is clear to everyone: Why reject pay? Because everyone in American should have the same opportunity for fair pay!

3. WISE AND FRUGAL

THOMAS JEFFERSON, FIRST INAUGURAL ADDRESS (1801)[1]

Keywords: frugal, government, metaphor, noble, list, unity, wise

Strategy: The Circle—Talk Principles—Law and Order

> ### Quote
> "If there be any among us who would wish to dissolve this Union or to change its republican form, let them stand undisturbed as monuments of the safety with which error of opinion may be tolerated where reason is left free to combat it. I know, indeed, that some honest men fear that a republican government can not be strong, that this Government is not strong enough; but would the honest patriot, in the full tide of successful experiment, abandon a government which has so far kept us free and firm on the theoretic and visionary fear that this Government, the world's best hope, may by possibility want energy to preserve itself? I trust not. I believe this, on the contrary, the strongest Government on earth. I believe it the only one where every man, at the call of the law, would fly to the standard of the law, and would meet invasions of the public order as his own personal concern. Sometimes it is said that man can not be trusted with the government of himself. Can he, then, be trusted with the government of others? Or have we found angels in the forms of

kings to govern him? Let history answer this question . . . Let us, then, with courage and confidence pursue our own Federal and Republican principles, our attachment to union and representative government. Kindly separated by nature and a wide ocean from the exterminating havoc of one quarter of the globe; too high-minded to endure the degradations of the others; possessing a chosen country, with room enough for our descendants to the thousandth and thousandth generation; entertaining a due sense of our equal right to the use of our own faculties, to the acquisitions of our own industry, to honor and confidence from our fellow-citizens, resulting not from birth, but from our actions and their sense of them; enlightened by a benign religion, professed, indeed, and practiced in various forms, yet all of them inculcating honesty, truth, temperance, gratitude, and the love of man; acknowledging and adoring an overruling Providence, which by all its dispensations proves that it delights in the happiness of man here and his greater happiness hereafter—with all these blessings, what more is necessary to make us a happy and a prosperous people? Still one thing more, fellow-citizens—a wise and frugal Government, which shall restrain men from injuring one another, shall leave them otherwise free to regulate their own pursuits of industry and improvement, and shall not take from the mouth of labor the bread it has earned. This is the sum of good government, and this is necessary to close the circle of our felicities."

ANALYSIS

When we look for the frame in a speech, it is often helpful to start by asking: Is a particular word being repeated over and over? Is that word being talked about in a certain way? Quite often, if we can figure out the keyword and the logic behind its use, we are well on our way to finding the frame.

In his first inaugural speech, Thomas Jefferson, repeated the word "government" thirteen times in a few paragraphs, a statistic that would be noteworthy for a presidential speech twice as long. And how he described government was peculiar indeed.

Consider, for example, the section of the speech where Jefferson recounts a long list of all the qualities and features that the United States has at its disposal. This list names every material, geographic, and demographic need a new nation could possible desire for a prosperous future. He paints an image of the perfect situation for a nation to thrive. "With all these blessings," Jefferson asked his audience rhetorically, "what more is necessary to make us a happy and a prosperous people?" His answer: a "wise and frugal government." What a peculiar phrase. But what is peculiar about it?

In describing government in this passage, Jefferson used a conceptual logic that most people would associate with descriptions of people, not with bureaucracies. Governments have offices, committees, legislative rules. We describe them as "efficient" or "well run"— terms that describe the way machines function. When we talk about people, by contrast, we employ words like "wise" and "frugal." What made Jefferson's descriptions of government leap off the page is the way he described a good American government as if it had the moral fortitude of a person. We have everything we need, but unless a "wise and frugal" government stands with us, we are lost. One can imagine the audience nodding their heads as they silently repeated Jefferson's idea in their own minds, "Of course . . . a wise and frugal government . . . that is exactly what we want standing with us." Jefferson was truly a master—perhaps *the* master—at framing the idea of government.

Describing government as a person is not the frame per se, but the metaphor that invokes the frame. To get at the frame, we must first think through the logic Jefferson presented to us. To describe government as "wise and frugal" was to talk of government not only as a person, but as an extraordinarily wise being capable of nurturing all of American politics, debate, and progress. Without that wise being, America would remain a collection of well-meaning people in a vast land filled with possibilities, but divided by irresolvable conflict. By contrast, under the watchful eye and wisdom of that great being, America could resolve its political disputes, achieve sustained national unity, and build a future of life and liberty.

So, it is not the metaphor that is the frame; the frame is the full, unspoken logic the metaphor opens onto. In this case, Jefferson's way of describing government in his speech invokes a logic remarkably close to the idea of the one being or God at the heart of monotheistic religions. It also invokes the idea of many beings in Greek mythology.

All of this adds up to "Wise Government" being the frame in the first major speech by Jefferson. Given the fierce anti-government rhetoric used by many American presidents since the 1980s, the high moral status and central role Jefferson affords government may come as a surprise to many contemporary readers.

The constitution was, of course, the most famous list of principles and virtues that Jefferson contributed to. But in his first inaugural speech, we are able to hear—for the first time with absolute clarity—how Jefferson invoked "Wise Government" as the key piece holding the whole American puzzle together. To create a "Wise Government," Jefferson recommended that Americans, of course, follow his list of principles.

There was good reason for Jefferson to have framed the speech in these terms. Having just finished a bitter election campaign in which the very principles of his Republican system of government were called into question, Jefferson seized upon his inauguration as a chance to reaffirm his vision.

Most people in the contemporary political scene only quote Jefferson for his famous "wall of separation" remark about the relationship between church and state. But his first inaugural speech demonstrates that the "wise government" frame has many more uses beyond the question of religion and American politics. Jefferson's inaugural speech is particularly valuable in light of the contemporary conservative idea that "government is the problem," as his speech demonstrates how a founding president talked about government as the key piece to ensuring life, liberty and happiness in American society.

STRATEGY

[Politician]—The Circle

When Jefferson talked about "wise government" as the key to American society, he did so using a memorable image that progressives can apply widely in debate: a circle. "This is the sum of good government," Jefferson said. "And this is necessary to close the circle of our felicities." In that statement, "the circle" is a complete and healthy American society that maintains conditions of liberty wherein individuals can pursue their own happiness according to their needs. While today's progressives should probably avoid the old-fashioned word "felicities," talking about society and government through this metaphor of "the circle" can be very effective.

However, even progressives, who believe deeply in good government as an essential structuring force in American society, have developed the unfortunate habit of apologizing for government programs instead of talking about government ideals. Once we follow Jefferson's example and imagine good government as the piece that completes the circle of a healthy American society, we are able to create new terms that can be used to express this idea in a variety of more specific debate areas. For example:

> Social Security is the key piece that completes the American system of liberty, freeing citizens in mind and body to live happy, confident lives.

In that statement, the metaphor of "the circle" is evoked by the phrase "key piece." Without Social Security (government), the circle is incomplete. Another example might involve the idea of being "within" the circle:

> In the absence of public education guaranteed by good government, many Americans will remain forever outside the promise of our Constitution.

The circle is a metaphor that allows progressives to talk about good government as including and completing our way of life and, by extension, to talk about bad government as excluding many and therefore leaving American society incomplete.

[Activist]—Talk Principles

A principle is a fundamental truth or proposition that serves as the foundation for a system of belief or behavior or for a chain of reasoning. What distinguishes a principle is its generality. If we say, "Americans believe in working together," we have stated a principle. How we plan bringing that principle to reality—actually working together—is a different story. A principle is like a plan, in other words, minus the details. Jefferson had a real flair for talking in principles, and progressives could benefit by following his example to help drive the contemporary debate.

Consider, for example, this string of "principles of our Government" that Jefferson unloaded on his audience halfway through his speech:

> Equal and exact justice to all men, of whatever state or persuasion, religious or political; peace, commerce, and honest friendship with all nations, entangling alliances with none; the support of the State governments in all their rights, as the most competent administrations for our domestic concerns and the surest bulwarks against antirepublican tendencies; the preservation of the General Government in its whole constitutional vigor, as the sheet anchor of our peace at home and safety abroad; a jealous care of the right of election by the people—a mild and safe corrective of abuses which are lopped by the sword of revolution where peaceable remedies are unprovided; absolute acquiescence in the decisions of the majority, the vital principle of republics, from which is no appeal but to force, the vital principle and immediate parent of despotism; a well-disciplined militia,

our best reliance in peace and for the first moments of war till regulars may relieve them; the supremacy of the civil over the military authority; economy in the public expense, that labor may be lightly burthened;[2] the honest payment of our debts and sacred preservation of the public faith; encouragement of agriculture, and of commerce as its handmaid; the diffusion of information and arraignment of all abuses at the bar of the public reason; freedom of religion; freedom of the press, and freedom of person under the protection of the habeas corpus, and trial by juries impartially selected.[3]

Jefferson called this list the "bright constellation" that guided America through the steps of revolution and reformation. Not only does this list still guide us today, but every progressive candidate, politician, staffer, activist and voter should tape Jefferson's "constellation" to their refrigerator door so they can see it and learn from it.

But how do we talk about principles? Unlike in Jefferson's day, it is best not to present the whole list of principles in speech, but to select three as they pertain to a given situation. For example, in a speech on foreign policy:

"America's foreign policy should always be based on honest friendship, peace at home, and safety abroad."

This is a shortened version of Jefferson's list that hits on the core principles of American government that pertain to a progressive vision of foreign commerce diplomacy and military policy. Another three principles might be used in a speech on fair elections, a key progressive issue:

"American government can only be complete when firmly grounded in the right of election by the people and open access to information."

Such a sentence could be a key part of a speech on the principles behind a paper receipt system in electronic voting machines. The key is to realize that principles are general: they are plans without the details. Therefore, even though Jefferson's list was penned in 1801, it can still help us today to understand what we mean, as well as how to say it better.

[Citizen]—Law And Order

In George Bush's nearly two terms in office, so many elected Republican officials and staffers have been charged with felonies that the American public has been faced almost constantly with questions about the lawlessness of their own government. Often, when the topic of criminal behavior of politicians comes up, the discussion turns to a general cynicism instead of a well-framed progressive discussion about the dangers that dishonest government poses to the country.

Jefferson's inaugural speech reminds us that to speak of the law is to speak of the greatest of all American principles: unity of the people. In the most contentious of all times, Jefferson explained, Americans "arranged themselves under the will of the law, and unite[d] in common efforts for the common good."

One way to frame the debate about progressive principle is to connect Jefferson to popular culture. For example, if the topic of government corruption comes up in conversation, one might respond:

> If Thomas Jefferson were alive, today, I am certain he would be a *Law and Order* junkie. He would be rolling in his grave if he knew about all these Republican criminal scandals plaguing the government he designed. Jefferson was totally convinced that respect for the law was the key to American unity. He would have seen corruption in government not just as a crime, but as a danger to the existence of the country.

Connecting Jefferson's idea of unity to a television show may feel a bit strange at first, but the reference keeps the focus of the discussion on progressive principles. In a more straightforward connection, perhaps, one might also mention that Jefferson would have also been a fan of Al Gore, as Gore spoke of unity and the law in his passionate 2005 "American Heresy" speech in support of the right to a Senate filibuster:

> As Aristotle once said of virtue, respect for the rule of law is "one thing." It is indivisible. And so long as it remains indivisible, so will our country. But if either major political party is ever so beguiled by a lust for power that it abandons this unifying principle, then the fabric of our democracy will be torn.[4]

Gore's use of the word "indivisible" was meant to remind his listeners of the pledge of allegiance, pretty much the only place any American ever hears or uses that word. But the principle of "unity under the law" clearly channeled Jefferson. And it offered a lesson to the type of language that any progressive can use to frame a speech on the idea of law as the core principle on which the unity of the American people depends.

4. OF THE PEOPLE

ABRAHAM LINCOLN, GETTYSBURG ADDRESS (1863)[1]

Keywords: action, ground, liberty, memory, message, sacrifice, war

Strategy: Dying in Vain—Talk about Service—Conversations about War

Quote

"Four score and seven years ago our fathers brought forth on this continent, a new nation, conceived in Liberty, and dedicated to the proposition that all men are created equal. Now we are engaged in a great civil war, testing whether that nation, or any nation so conceived and so dedicated, can long endure. We are met on a great battle-field of that war. We have come to dedicate a portion of that field, as a final resting place for those who here gave their lives that that nation might live. It is altogether fitting and proper that we should do this. But, in a larger sense, we can not dedicate—we can not consecrate—we can not hallow—this ground. The brave men, living and dead, who struggled here, have consecrated it, far above our poor power to add or detract. The world will little note, nor long remember what we say here, but it can never forget what they did here. It is for us the living, rather, to be dedicated here to the unfinished work which they who fought here have thus far so nobly advanced. It is rather for us to be here dedicated to the great task remaining before us—that from these honored dead we take increased devotion to that cause for which they gave the last full measure of devotion—that we here highly resolve that these dead shall not have died in vain—that this nation, under God, shall have a new birth of freedom—and that government of the people, by the people, for the people, shall not perish from the earth."

ANALYSIS

The Gettysburg Address, delivered to consecrate a national cemetery for soldiers who were killed in one of the bloodiest battles of the civil war,[2] is probably the most famous three paragraphs ever spoken by a President and contains what is, arguably, the most memorized opening line of American rhetoric. Lincoln was the premier American wordsmith, and most of us have heard this speech so many times that its very words seem to bubble up from within us. However, what makes Lincoln's speech so remarkable is not just his phrasing, but his framing. This is the point where many people get confused because they mistake the frame of the speech for the message, but they are two very different things.

To find the message in any presidential address, it is helpful to imagine that every speech comes with a little note attached telling the audience—in a single sentence—the big idea in the speech. If we imagine that the Gettysburg Address had such a note attached to it, this is what Lincoln would have written as his important big idea:

Actions speak louder than words

Easy, right? Most of us probably wrote a middle school essay on that very idea. Even as kids, we could all understand the message of Lincoln's speech because it is a basic, American idea. But Lincoln did not actually utter the phrase "actions speak louder than words"; instead he delivered the following more stylized phrase:

> The world will little note, nor long remember what we say here, but it can never forget what they did here.

The language is a little old-fashioned, but we can still see the message clearly—"actions speak louder than words." It is also fascinating to note that this message comes exactly halfway through the speech—an almost perfectly placed piece of rhetoric. The message also expresses a clear, moral point. Politicians can talk about the importance of sacrifice for their country, Lincoln explains, but those words will never come close to the self-sacrifice of citizens themselves. The memory of soldiers who fall in battle in defense of a nation "conceived in Liberty" and dedicated to equality will stir our hearts for generations. Lincoln was telling his audience that the words of politicians—his words—were at best road signs on the map of history. It is what we do that matters most. And what did Lincoln want everyone who was listening to him that day to do? Win the war!

So, if that was the message in Lincoln's speech, what was the frame? Before we answer that question, it helps to think about the difference between a message and a frame. A message is explicit and a frame is implicit. We can actually hear or read the message, but the frame is left largely unspoken. Instead, a frame is invoked by certain keywords that call to mind a particular logic in the mind of the listener or reader. While remaining unsaid, the frame nonetheless guides how we understand what we are hearing.

To find the message, we need to look for the most important sentence or phrase. To find the frame, by contrast, we need to first pose a few questions about the speech, collect some keywords, and then give voice to the unspoken logic that orders the entire speech. In particular, we need to look for any words that are repeated in a noticeable way, as framers repeat words in speeches not only to invoke the frame, but to draw our attention to it.

Looking over the Gettysburg Address, it is not hard to find the point in the speech where a keyword is repeated in a noteworthy manner:

government of the people, by the people, for the people

Lincoln repeated the word "people" three times in a row at the end of the speech to emphasize the broad frame he had invoked in the very first line: we the people. The "We the People" frame is the broad logic that defines a "nation," "country," or "government" as a group of people. It originates in the first words of the Declaration of Independence, and is the logical basis for the fundamental American values of unity, representation, and equality.

Today, far from the struggles of the Civil War, it is easy for most Americans to see our nation as a group of people gathered around a common set of ideas and principles, as opposed to just a piece of land. But in the throes of the Civil War, Lincoln knew that a principle-oriented understanding of nationhood had begun to give way to a crude "protect our turf" point of view. The larger point in the Gettysburg Address, in other words, was not about land—even if it was land Lincoln was dedicating with the speech—but about defense of principle, and the people who lived by them, as the very reason for fighting wars. As Lincoln framed the debate, the deaths of the Civil War took place on multiple battlefields, but the broad struggle unfolded over a single idea: a nation based on equality. War, thus, was about the preservation—and perseverance—of "We the People" as a frame through which Americans would view their past and their future.

Right from the start, Lincoln used words and images that invoked "We The People," thereby framing the discussion of battlefields and soldiers as a conversation about preserving the people's democracy. "Look," Lincoln was saying, "eighty-seven years ago, the people who founded this nation stood on a piece of land just like we are today. But the nation they founded was not about that land. It was about this new idea that all people were equal. And the longer we fight this war, the more we risk forgetting that basic idea of 'We the People.'"

When Lincoln ended the speech by repeating the "of the people, for the people" line, his audience understood it as a reference to the principle of equality, because he had invoked that frame in just about every line of the speech. And the power of this frame persists to this day.

Many Americans think of the Gettysburg Address as too formal and to be of use today. But that is a mistake. The Gettysburg Address is full of tools that can be used to advance progressive ideas about America in a time of war. The trick is not to confuse the speaking style with the message or the frame. Lincoln's style may be a product of the past, but his ideas can carry us forward to the future.

STRATEGY

[Politician]—Dying In Vain

Since the invasion of Iraq, Republicans have repeatedly invoked Lincoln's idea that "these dead shall not have died in vain." Unfortunately, Lincoln never intended his idea to be used as a justification for an aggressive war, but to advance the progressive American values of unity and equality in a time of war.

Reclaiming the true intent of Lincoln's words can be an important strategy for progressives when speaking against the occupation of Iraq and when critiquing the doctrine of preemptive war. The key is to follow Lincoln's lead and first invoke the "We the People" frame. When speaking on the floor of the House or Senate, for example, a progressive politician might say:

> The United States is a nation founded on one core principle: 'we the people.' We are a nation that views all people as equal and unified. It is our history. It is our legacy. It is our nation. And the purpose of our military is to defend that principle. But if we allow our military to be used to achieve

other goals—for example, to extend American power in the world along ideological lines—then it will be as if all the American heroes who ever fought and died in defense of 'we the people'—who died in defense of the American people—will have died in vain. Because an aggressive war, a war of preemption, is first and foremost a betrayal of American principle. And when we abandon American principle, we are saying that all who died defending us have died in vain.

This is just one example of how to use Lincoln's frame to advance a progressive vision of the military in critique of the Bush Doctrine. In addition, channeling Lincoln is incredibly empowering. Even if an elected official ultimately does not use Lincoln's exact frame or phrases, drawing on the Gettysburg Address to understand how to speak about American values in a time of war can be a very important first step toward delivering a persuasive progressive speech.

[Activist] - Talk About Service

For activists, the Gettysburg Address offers a strategy for being persuasive in debates about the military. Too often, progressives reduce their views on the military down to the formulaic cliché, "I support the troops, but I am against the war." That is not a persuasive statement, and smacks of political fear and calculation, even if progressives are sincere. A better approach is for progressives to speak with conviction about the importance of service.

Speaking about "service" when progressives talk about the military is one way to invoke Lincoln's message that "actions speak louder than words." Americans sign up for the military, not to support a policy position, but because they are dedicated to the idea of service—in other words, to the idea that actions are more important than words. While not all progressives dedicate themselves to service specifically by enlisting in the armed forces, progressivism is rooted deeply in Lincoln's principle that actions are more important than words. Each and every discussion of the military can be viewed as an opportunity to express admiration for those who serve and to reiterate the importance of service to the country. For example, in a conversation with a voter about Iraq, a progressive activist might say:

> Look, there is nothing more important to America than the dedication to service of men and women serving in the armed forces. Their service—their action—is far more important than any words spoken by any politician. And when I look at the approach to national defense over the past five years, I see a set of policies that have fundamentally undermined that dedication to service.

What a different conversation this initiates! When a progressive discussion of the military begins by engaging the idea of service, it instantly has more power—and more sincerity—than a similar conversation begun with the habitually repeated "I support the troops." Suddenly, the progressive activist is not so much critiquing the actions of the military as speaking out in defense of the integrity of an American principle.

In time of war, evoking "service" becomes that much more important for progressive activists because our dedication to service during war is heightened by the very idea that Lincoln discussed in the Gettysburg Address: the sacredness of an action in defense of the nation when it results in death. That sacrifice, as Lincoln put it, "consecrates" the nation. And so to do anything but express admiration for it—and humility in the face of it—is tantamount to desecration, which will make people uncomfortable, even if they cannot explain why.

[Citizen]—Conversations About War

One of the great anxieties progressives experience is the dreaded dinner table conversation with a Republican relative about "the war." In these situations, when we are asked what we think about the war, most progressives say something to the effect of, "I am against the occupation in Iraq" and "against the President's policy." While that seems like the right thing to say, we lose the debate the moment somebody asks, "What would you do, then, cut and run?" Why do we always lose at this point? Because we choose to talk about policy when the debate is really about principle. And since we are not experts on military policy, we stumble when asked about our policy. Even if we do provide an answer (e.g. "Withdraw troops incrementally starting next month, redirect the funds saved on the deployment to humanitarian aid") our answers rarely carry much weight. We are not generals, after all.

Believe it or not, the Gettysburg Address can be incredibly useful in changing the entire dynamic of these kinds of discussions because it teaches us to frame debates about war in terms of principle, not policy. War policy is for war strategists. Our concern is to ground the debate in a discussion of clear progressive principles and keep it there. We might start off, for example, by saying this:

I am opposed to the war on principle.

It is such a simple line, and it is what every progressive believes—but we never say it. But what is our principle of war that leads us to oppose or support a given military action? Lincoln tells us:

that government of the people, by the people, for the people shall not perish from the earth

Ultimately, that is the principle by which we support or oppose a war fought by American soldiers. We can then refer back to this basic principle to lead the discussion and not simply react to questions.

When we were attacked on September 11, 2001, for example, reacting with military force against the attackers was a principled action. And that is why progressives almost uniformly supported the war against Osama Bin Laden's camps in Afghanistan. But then the

Bush administration chose to wage a second war that was clearly against principle. And they did it by advancing a different principle for war that most Americans had never considered before. To address this alarming change in our military policy—from defense to preemptive offense—progressives might say the following:

> America has only ever declared war to defend the government of the people, by the people, for the people—but never as a preemptive policy based on the suspicion that a foreign nation might at some point in the future attack us.
>
> Since this country was founded, we have always fought wars for one reason. And if we change the reason we fight wars, then we have also changed our country—and that change cannot stand.

Once we are talking in terms of the American principle of defending "government of the people" as the basis for military action, the force of Lincoln's ideas inform our words, and help drive the debate towards a progressive vision. So now, if asked, "What would you do, cut and run?" the response is easy:

> That is not really the point. Since we have sacrificed the very principles that America stands for, we simply cannot continue this occupation and still be true to American ideals.

Now, obviously we cannot go into every conversation with a memorized script that we pull out whenever the word "Iraq" or "war" comes up. Rather, we simply need to remember the key phrase "principle, not policy" as our starting point. After that, we should be able to improvise with confidence, and lead a discussion that is far more interesting and far more progressive than even your most Republican of relatives will have anticipated.

5. THE MUCK RAKE

THEODORE ROOSEVELT, ADDRESS ON THE CORNERSTONE LAYING FOR THE CANNON BUILDING (1906)[1]

Keywords: character, corruption, cleaning up, cynicism, lies, progress

Strategy: Corruption and Character—Talk about Honesty— Looking Up

Quote

"In Bunyan's *Pilgrim's Progress* you may recall the description of the man with the muck rake, the man who could look no way but downward, with the muck rake in his hand; who was offered a celestial crown for his muck rake, but who would neither look up nor regard the crown he was offered, but continued to rake to himself the filth of the floor.

In *Pilgrim's Progress* the man with the muck rake is set forth as the example of him whose vision is fixed on carnal instead of spiritual things. Yet he also typifies the man who in this life consistently refuses to see aught that is lofty, and fixes his eyes with solemn intentness only on that which is vile and debasing.

Now, it is very necessary that we should not flinch from seeing what is vile and debasing. There is filth on the floor, and it must be scraped up with the muck rake; and there are times and places where this service is the most needed of all the services that can be performed. But the man who never does anything else, who never thinks or speaks or writes, save of his feats with the muck rake, speedily becomes, not a help but one of the most potent forces for evil.

There are in the body politic, economic and social, many and grave evils, and there is urgent necessity for the sternest war upon them. There should be relentless exposure of and attack upon every evil man, whether politician or business man, every evil practice, whether in politics, business, or social life. I hail as a benefactor every writer or speaker, every man who, on the platform or in a book, magazine, or newspaper, with merciless severity makes such attack, provided always that he in his turn remembers that the attack is of use only if it is absolutely truthful.

The liar is no whit better than the thief, and if his mendacity takes the form of slander he may be worse than most thieves. It puts a premium upon knavery untruthfully to attack an honest man, or even with hysterical exaggeration to assail a bad man with untruth.

An epidemic of indiscriminate assault upon character does no good, but very great harm. The soul of every scoundrel is gladdened whenever an honest man is assailed, or even when a scoundrel is untruthfully assailed.

Now, it is easy to twist out of shape what I have just said, easy to affect to misunderstand it, and if it is slurred over in repetition not difficult really to misunderstand it. Some persons are sincerely incapable of understanding that to denounce mud slinging does not mean the endorsement of whitewashing; and both the interested individuals who need whitewashing and those others who practice mud slinging like to encourage such confusion of ideas.

ANALYSIS

If Teddy Roosevelt were alive today, he would take one look at the corruption scandals that have plagued the Republican Party in recent years and say, "This is exactly what I cautioned you against!" Even though the speech was delivered on the pretext of drumming up support for expanding the amount of office space in Washington, D.C., Roosevelt's famous "man with the muck rake" address is a take-no-prisoners warning on the threat that corruption posed to the American national character. And no president framed the concept of corruption with more clarity and power than Teddy Roosevelt. The "muck rake" speech was his attempt to redefine in the public's mind the significance of corruption and to reframe the entire political debate so that it would move forward under the broad banner of progress.

But what was the problem with corruption in the first place? In Roosevelt's time, the national debate defined corruption in material terms. In fact, we all know Teddy Roosevelt as the father of the "Square Deal," a proponent of stronger antitrust laws, and the great enforcer of controls on the increasingly powerful, turn-of-the-century industrial corporation. As President, he issued forty-four lawsuits against major corporations, passed measures reining in the virtually unlimited power of the railroad companies, and forced Congress to pass basic legislation requiring the labeling of food. Despite all the material controls that Roosevelt created and enforced, he believed that corruption was first and foremost a spiritual threat to the character of the nation.

The significance of the "muck rake" speech lay in Roosevelt's ability to rip "corruption" from the unspoken materialist logic that had defined it up to that point in American political rhetoric and to redefine it in terms of national character. He achieved this remarkable feat by drawing on a well-known passage from *The Pilgrim's Progress* (1678), a classic of moral literature written by John Bunyan.[2] Quoting classic literature is not something that we now associate with presidential speeches, but Roosevelt used the "filth on the floor" frame from Bunyan to reframe the idea of corruption in spiritual terms.

Often, a President will invoke a frame by using a particularly resonant metaphor that helps people understand an otherwise abstract idea. That is what Roosevelt did with the image of the man with the muck rake. When we read that passage, we see how "filth on the floor" becomes a metaphor for corruption. Even though corruption is a complex series of business and political actions that needs to be controlled and stopped by innovative legislation and enforcement, Roosevelt talked about corruption as if it were simple "filth on the floor" that could be raked up. What an incredibly powerful idea. But that was just the beginning of Roosevelt's frame.

Once his audience heard him talk about "corruption" as "filth on the floor," their instinct would have been to advocate "raking" it all up—a logical extension of the frame. But Roosevelt warned them that:

> the Man with the Muck Rake is set forth as the example of him whose vision is fixed on carnal instead of spiritual things. Yet he also typifies the man who in this life consistently refuses to see aught that is lofty, and fixes his eyes with solemn intentness only on that which is vile and debasing.

Roosevelt was seeking to do far more than enlist the public to use every means at their disposal—the press, the law, business practices—to rid the political and corporate system of corruption; he was trying to inspire the public to end corruption through the virtues of honesty and truth. Roosevelt understood that a system beset with corruption was bound to infect the national character with a generalized attitude of cynicism that would undermine any attempts at reform, and he was concerned about an America so totally focused on cleaning up corruption that it saw corruption in everything. Even good projects, good business practices and good politicians would be tainted by the never-ending quest to get rid of corruption, to the point where people would lie to indict a thief. A corrupt system, in Roosevelt's view, gave rise to a national character than had no faith or trust in the very institutions it sought to reclaim. And this distrust was even worse for the long-term health of American character than the crimes being prosecuted. We can think of it this way: once we set about cleaning the "filth on the floor," the filth gets on everything. So, if the goal is ultimately to have a clean system, how do we do it?

The answer Roosevelt provided was elegant and visionary: Look up! In the "filth on the floor" frame, the great moral focus guiding the cleaning up of corruption are the great ideas of truth and honesty, which Roosevelt saw as the spiritual and ethical purpose of American character:

> We appreciate that the things of the body are important, but we appreciate also that the things of the soul are immeasurably more important. The foundation stone of national life is, and ever must be, the high individual character of the average citizen.

The image of national life having a "foundation stone" made of the "high individual character of the average citizen" is itself built on the logic of the "filth on the floor" frame. We clean the floor not to remain mired in muck, but to clear away the residue of immorality and untruth from the "foundation stone" of American national life.

And if Roosevelt's audience was listening closely that day, they would have noticed that he began his speech with a call to construct new buildings for an expanded national capital in Washington, D.C., and ended by tying the architectural concept of a "foundation stone" to the idea of national character itself. Tackling corruption without being drawn into an endless obsession with evil, Roosevelt was telling us, will allow us to focus on the lofty task of building a new and glorious capital city as a living monument to American national character. For that very reason, the "muck rake" is the one speech that every Washington, D.C. lobbyist should be forced to read.

STRATEGY

[Politician]—Corruption and Character

During the presidency of George W. Bush, there have been enough political and corporate corruption scandals to make even Teddy Roosevelt blush. Enron, WorldCom, Jack Abramoff, Tom Delay, Plamegate, Randy Cunningham, Bob Ney, David Safavian, Mark Foley—the list goes on and on. To frame these Republican scandals for the 2006 midterm elections, Democrats spoke about a Republican "culture of corruption." And in fact, the "culture of corruption" frame was a key factor leading to the sweeping success Democrats enjoyed at both a state and federal level. Looking beyond the individual scandals—and looking ahead to future campaigns—one way to extend the persuasive "culture of corruption" frame could be for progressives to engage the much broader idea of American character.

As Roosevelt's "filth on the floor" frame defines the issue, the problem with corruption extends far beyond the crimes committed. The danger is that persistent corruption threatens to poison American character with cynicism and blind obsession with material concerns, eliminating interest in "aught that is lofty." For example, a progressive Democrat in office or on the campaign trail, when talking about the Republican lobbying scandals, could say something along these lines:

> Each individual corrupted by a lobbying scandal constitutes a terrible crime and an immoral act. But the crimes alone are not the greatest threat posed by corruption scandals such as this one. The greatest threat is to America's national character. It is a threat because we have no choice but to confront this corruption, but to do so is to risk dropping our heads in cynicism and contempt for such lofty ideals as service, honesty and representation. Corruption in government, corruption in corporate practices—these are not just crimes, but a cycle that must be broken to protect the ideals that serve as the moral cornerstone of every individual American.

Notice how the "filth on the floor" frame provides a basic logic for linking lobbying reform to a much broader set of national ideals. The message in this potential speech clip is not that the crimes themselves, but that we risk "dropping our heads." That image draws directly on Roosevelt's technique of framing the abstract notion of corruption through the actions and gestures of an allegorical character who "cleans up" the floor."

[Activist]—Talk about Honesty

The power of the word "honesty" is a key lesson for progressive activists to take from Roosevelt's speech.

Often, as activists are drawn into the hand-to-hand combat of a campaign's ground battle, they find themselves tangled up in a he-said-she-said shouting match centered around accusations that one campaign lied about the actions of another.

In a recent example of this, the progressive activists working on the Ned Lamont campaign in the 2006 Connecticut Democratic primary were accused by the Joe Lieberman campaign of crashing the Lieberman website on the eve of the primary.[3] In response, the Lamont activists accused the Lieberman team of lying.[4] To this day, even thought it is clear that the Lieberman site crashed for technical reasons and not as a result of dirty tricks, the tit-for-tat argument over who lied to who remained a sore point that inevitably soured some voters on the race.

To take a stronger, more effect approach to this problem, the Lamont team could have framed their responses to this incident in terms of "honesty" rather than "lies." Here is an example of how that might have sounded:

> Honesty is not just a cornerstone of American character, it is the ideal on which this Senate campaign was built. Honest dialogue with the voters of Connecticut. Honest debate of our national policies at home and abroad. Honest work for

real change in leadership. We believe the Lieberman website went down on Tuesday night for reasons having only to do with the campaign's choice of Internet service and the level of web traffic. To suggest otherwise is to question the honesty of this campaign and to put accusations ahead of the ideals of Connecticut voters.

One thing to keep in mind when faced with a scandal of this sort is that the word "lie" draws people's attention back to the events in question, and tangles them in the argument. The word "honesty," by contrast, lifts people's heads "up" to a "lofty ideal" embodied by a progressive candidate. This was Roosevelt's broader point in the "muck rake" speech: to not allow the important task of facing down corruption to drag us down at the level of character.

To avoid being drawn down and to lead the debate forward, activists can respond to accusations with appeals to "honesty" rather than counter with accusations of lies.

[Citizen]—Looking Up

In everyday conversations about politics, progressive voters often find themselves talking at a different level than Republicans do. Progressives by nature like to talk about "issues" and "policies" even though what draws them to progressive candidates are principles. But sometimes, talking about principles can be a bit too formal for everyday conversation. How often do we find ourselves talking about "peace, commerce and honest friendship" while chatting with a friend at a fast food restaurant?

How, then, can we open up a place in everyday conversation to express a progressive belief in principles? Roosevelt's speech provides a great answer to this question. We can use the metaphor "looking up" as a road sign in our conversation—a signal to the other person that we have a set of bigger ideas to talk about if they are willing to join us in that discussion.

We use "road signs" all the time in conversation. When we talk on the telephone, for example, we don't just hang up when we are done with what we have to say. Instead, we put out a road sign, "Well, it was great talking to you," or "Alright, now." After we put out one of these road signs, the person at the other end of the line knows that you are ready to end the conversation and that the word "goodbye" followed by a mutual hanging up of phones will come next. (The next time you talk on the phone, try withholding the road sign when you are ready to hang up. The discomfort you feel will tell you how important road signs are in everyday speech).

To draw people into a discussion of principles, it can help greatly to provide them a road sign, and Roosevelt's phrase "looking up" in his "muck rake" speech provides the perfect conversation starter. For example, imagine you are talking current events or politics with a friend and you want to tell them why you like a progressive candidate. Your friend asks, "What are her positions?" Since you know you like the candidate because of her principles, you might say this to your friend:

> The issues are a big part of why I support her as a candidate. But leaving the issues on the floor, let's look up for a second.

And then pause. "Looking up" in this instance is a road sign to your friend that you are about to talk about something larger, more important—"aught that is lofty." "Looking up" as a road sign accomplishes two things that are consistent with what Roosevelt achieved in the "muck rake" speech: it distinguishes between material and "lofty" concerns, and it defines politics as a question of individual character. And that is what we want in our conversations with friends. We want them to see, and understand, that the choice to support a progressive candidate is about principle, the cornerstone on which all issues reside.

6. HIGHWAYS OF THE WORLD

WOODROW WILSON, WAR MESSAGE (1917)[1]

Keywords: danger, freedom, highway, international, security

Strategy: Reason for War—Danger We Face—Thinking Big

Quote

"On the 3d of February last I officially laid before you the extraordinary announcement of the Imperial German Government that on and after the 1st day of February it was its purpose to put aside all restraints of law or of humanity and use its submarines to sink every vessel that sought to approach either the ports of Great Britain and Ireland or the western coasts of Europe or any of the ports controlled by the enemies of Germany within the Mediterranean. That had seemed to be the object of the German submarine warfare earlier in the war, but since April of last year the Imperial Government had somewhat restrained the commanders of its undersea craft in conformity with its promise then given to us that passenger boats should not be sunk and that due warning would be given to all other vessels which its submarines might seek to destroy, when no resistance was offered or escape attempted, and care taken that their crews were given at least a fair chance to save their lives in their open boats. The precautions taken were meager and haphazard enough, as was proved in distressing instance after instance in the progress of the cruel and unmanly business, but a certain degree of restraint was observed The new policy has swept every restriction aside. Vessels of every kind, whatever their flag, their character, their cargo, their destination, their errand, have been ruthlessly sent to the bottom without warning and without thought of help or mercy for those on board, the vessels of friendly neutrals along with those of belligerents. Even hospital ships and ships carrying relief to the sorely bereaved and stricken people of Belgium, though the latter were provided with safe-conduct through the proscribed areas by the German Government itself and were distinguished by unmistakable marks of identity, have been sunk with the same reckless lack of compassion or of principle.

I was for a little while unable to believe that such things would in fact be done by any government that had hitherto subscribed to the humane practices of civilized nations. International law had its origin in the attempt to set up some law which would be respected and observed upon the seas, where no nation had right of dominion and where lay the free highways of the world. By painful stage after stage has that law been built up, with meagre enough results, indeed, after all was accomplished that could be accomplished, but always with a clear view, at least, of what the heart and conscience of mankind demanded. This minimum of right the German Government has swept aside under the plea of retaliation and necessity and because it had no weapons which it could use at sea except these which it is impossible to employ as it is employing them without throwing to the winds all scruples of humanity or of respect for the understandings that were supposed to underlie the intercourse of the world. I am not now thinking of the loss of property involved, immense and serious as that is, but only of the wanton and wholesale destruction of the lives of noncombatants, men, women, and children, engaged in pursuits which have always, even in the darkest periods of modern history, been deemed innocent and legitimate. Property can be paid for; the lives of peaceful and innocent people can not be. The present German submarine warfare against commerce is a warfare against mankind.

It is a war against all nations. American ships have been sunk, American lives taken, in ways which it has stirred us very deeply to learn of, but the ships and people of other neutral and friendly nations have been sunk and overwhelmed in the waters in the same way. There has been no discrimination. The challenge is to all mankind. Each nation must decide for itself how it will meet it. The choice we make for ourselves must be made with a moderation of counsel and a temperateness of judgment befitting our character and our motives as a nation. We must put excited feeling away. Our motive will not be revenge or the victorious assertion of the physical might of the nation, but only the vindication of right, of human right, of which we are only a single champion."

ANALYSIS

A speech designed to persuade the nation to declare war on another country is perhaps the gravest of all presidential subjects. Nowadays, we live in a post-Cold War state of readiness, meaning that we always have a fully staffed, fully equipped army standing at the ready. In fact, because our military has been built up with the threat of nuclear attack in mind, the American military is always a "button push" away from launching an attack.

When President Woodrow Wilson delivered his now famous "War Message" to Congress in 1917, the military situation of the United States was completely different than it is today. Back then, if the country decided to go to war, it needed to draft military personnel, build equipment, and manufacture munitions. Because of the sheer size and scope of taking the country to war, the effort involved a massive public and private coordination. Industry and government needed to align in such a way that people's lives would be instantly and irrevocably altered, a vast collective commitment that Franklin Roosevelt would later call "shared sacrifice." In this context, a President taking the country to war had to make the case that the danger that needed to be confronted was worthy of a massive change in the everyday lives of citizens.

At the heart of Wilson's message is "the seas" as a metaphor for peace, freedom and cooperation between nations:

> International law had its origin in the attempt to set up some law which would be respected and observed upon the seas, where no nation had right of dominion and where lay the free highways of the world.[2]

Wilson's idea of the seas as "free highways of the world" was a perfect metaphor for international cooperation. Since the sea is a means of transport open to all nations, for a country to threaten this free "highway" was to pose a potential danger to the entire world.

And what form did that danger present in Wilson's speech? Submarines. In fact, what Wilson did with German submarines in his speech was similar to what Stephen Spielberg would later do to great white sharks in the movie *Jaws*: He made them seem terrifying.

But beyond the image of the submarines as a dangerous threat lurking beneath dark waters, the power of Wilson's speech lay in his ability to frame danger as a threat to the core American principle of free and open transport on international waters. The German submarines were not merely a mortal threat to passengers on boats, or a material threat to property that was being transported, but a moral threat to the principle of free commerce, free movement, and free exchange between nations. Such a threat, Wilson emphasized, was not merely a danger to one nation, but to the entire world. Therefore, the war that every citizen in the United States would be joining was not simply a war between America and Germany, but "a war against all nations." It was, in other words, a World War.

Think about how different Wilson's speech would have been if he just said, "International waterways are defined as free and open according to international law. Germany broke the law when it attacked our ships. Therefore, the United States declares war on Germany." When reduced to this more mundane message, it becomes easier to see exactly how Wilson's frame transformed a declaration of war into a moment that galvanized the nation into action.

In what historians would later see as a startling transformation from his initial attempts to keep the country isolated from the conflict in Europe, Wilson's speech framed both Germany and the United States in terms that made going to war a moral choice.[3] In this quote from midway in the speech, Wilson even used imagery we often associate with the American Western frontier to make his case against Germany:

> Because submarines are in effect outlaws when used as the German submarines have been used against merchant shipping, it is impossible to defend ships against their attacks as the law of nations has assumed that merchantmen would defend themselves against privateers or cruisers, visible craft giving chase upon the open sea.[4]

This powerful statement reflected Wilson's changing view about getting involved in the war, as he was essentially saying, "Last year, I did not want to go to war. Now I do." And he framed that basic idea by defining German submarines as "outlaws"—outlaws that needed to be stopped before their unlawful actions brought about the total destruction of the basic American principles of free and open commerce, respect for international waters, and the right to defend person and property.

At this moment in American politics, rethinking how progressives talk about war is particularly germane. Our national debate has been overwhelmed in the past few elections by endless talk of threats to "freedom" and the need to use the military to attack potential dangers before they attack us. However, as the 2006 midterm elections showed, this preemptive approach to taking the nation to war has left a majority of Americans deeply troubled that our military has not only been used to violate core American principles, but that it has also been pulled away from the true dangers threatening our safety, security and ideals. President Wilson's 1917 "War Message" offers some key framing insights to help progressives once again lead the debate on national security.

STRATEGY

[Politician]—Reason For War

A clearly articulated, well-defined principle is the missing element in progressive efforts to lead the debate on national security. In this respect, Wilson's speech provides much more than a lesson in how to declare war—it shows how to frame a national security vision in terms of a threat to American principles.

During the Bush administration, national security has been dominated by a constant focus on the dangers we face through a repetition of the word "terrorism." But the principles under threat by that danger have never been linked to our military action in Iraq. In the place of defending American principles, President Bush has presented multiple arguments for the war through a series of shifting, and often false, premises, all gathered under the vague rubric of "freedom." And, as recent election results have demonstrated, rather than standing behind our military policy in Iraq, Americans are concerned that that policy has no clear purpose and, as such, must change drastically in order to protect us from the dangers we face.

Progressives can begin to reframe the national security debate by considering the similarities between the current security threats posed to air travel and the threats to sea travel posed in Wilson's time. As Americans, we believe today in the same principle of open travel and commerce as we believed in 1917—that the air, like the sea, is and should remain "free highways of the world." When our planes were hijacked and crashed into buildings in 2001, the principle of free highways was violated, but with one key difference: it was not one country that broke this principle, but an ideological group spread across many countries.

To frame the debate on national security in these terms, a progressive candidate or elected official might say:

> On September 11, 2001, our country witnessed an attack not only on the American people, but on a basic American principle: that government can and must guarantee the safety of its citizens. In previous years, attacks such as these seemed to be the criminal actions of a few extremists using bombs to wage politics. Now, we understand that these crimes are a systematic effort to undermine the confidence of the people in government itself by turning ordinary aspects of our everyday lives—ships, airplanes, trains—into dangerous weapons.

Notice how this statement defines the core problem of September 11 not by repeating the word "terrorist" or "terrorism," but by focusing on the principle at risk: government's ability to protect its citizens. The ability to name the threat, but then move the discussion to principle rather then a constant repetition of the danger is a core lesson from Wilson's speech.

Once the principle is defined, the approach to defending that principle from what threatens it is relatively simple to state:

> To fight this attack, we cannot simply declare war, because our enemy seeks not to bring down our nation or even a network of allied nations, but to destroy the very principles on which modern nations are based. Rather than declaring war, we must declare allegiance, we must declare unity, and we must declare collaboration. We must work together with every nation, first to find and stop those who plot to undermine our principles, then to build institutions that prevent their return.

In this way, Wilson's "War Message" offers an approach to defining a broad vision of what it means for the nation to be secure, not just a template for declaring war.

[Activist]—Danger We Face

Whereas progressive candidates and elected officials tend to talk about the national security dangers that America faces, but not the American principles that are under threat, progressive activists tend to critique current policies, but never talk about the actual dangers we face as a nation. As a result, progressive activists, while effective at raising awareness about the weaknesses or immorality of a particular war or policy, are not effective at persuading the public to be concerned about the actual security threats we face as a nation. In the case of the current occupation in Iraq, while progressive activists have been very effective at pointing out that the policy is misguided and reckless, their efforts could be doubled by drawing from Wilson's technique of naming the danger we face as a nation.

As part of a large-scale protest aimed at persuading the public to speak out against the U.S. war and occupation in Iraq, activists might address the crowd with a message along these lines:

> The war and occupation in Iraq are not just misguided, not just based on false claims, not just mismanaged and without any accountability for mistakes—but also leave us more vulnerable to danger.

> What is that danger? Attacks on innocent people doing nothing more than moving about on the free highways of our world.

> Since the war began, there have been more plots against planes.

> Since the war began, there have been more attacks on trains.

Since the war began, there have been more people recruited to kill the innocent.

We must stop this war because as a result of this war, the very people who seek to harm us have become more active, more creative, more emboldened, and—worst of all—better concealed than they were before we entered Iraq.

This is just one example of how a progressive protest speech to a large audience might frame a critique of the Iraq war in terms of the dangers we face as a nation.

Of course, at any protest, the success of the day often depends less on the speech than on the few words chanted over and over by an energetic crowd, or that single sentence printed quickly on handheld signs. How can a protest slogan critique the Bush policy in Iraq and talk about the dangers we face—all in a few words? These examples take their inspiration from the framing logic in the Wilson "War Message" and can be quickly adapted by a protest organizer:

- More Iraq means MORE ATTACKS!
- Another Year, MORE FEAR!
- More war, LESS SAFE!
- Fighting there, MORE FEAR HERE!

Ultimately, an organizer needs to write a slogan for a protest that fits the vision of the organization. But these starting points adapt the lessons of Wilson's framing techniques to a pressing contemporary concern of progressive activists: persuading the public, and politicians, to speak out more strongly against the current U.S. policy in Iraq. While the 2006 midterm elections were a good start in this direction, using Wilson's framing techniques can help us to increase these efforts.

Even more importantly, framing a protest in terms of the Iraqi occupation causing more danger at home redresses one of the key tactics used by conservatives to justify the war and occupation in Iraq: the idea that we are "fighting them there, so we don't have to fight them here." In fact, since we started "fighting them there" (in Iraq), the need to fight them here has become increasingly apparent. Framing a protest with that logic presents a powerful message.

[Citizen]—Thinking Big

One of the most powerful aspects of Wilson's "War Message" was his framing of German aggression on the seas as "a war against all nations." Too often, when discussing the current U.S. war in Iraq with relatives or friends who hold conservative political opinions, individual progressives talk only about their own personal views, saying "I am against the war" or "I believe this is wrong" or "I do not agree with this policy." Now, we are not Presidents standing before a joint session of Congress charged with the grave and historic responsibility of convincing the nation to enter World War I. Nonetheless, progressives often lose dinner table debates about the war and occupation in Iraq not because their understanding of the events is off target, but because they argue "too small."

To frame and control the debate, we must start by arguing big. Arguing "big" means arguing to set the terms of the debate—framing the debate—rather than simply charging in with one point to score and defend over and over again. But how can we argue big when the topic is war?

Wilson's "War Message" gives us an excellent example. In the speech, Wilson told his audience that, one year before the message he was delivering, he had believed that the best way to approach the mounting conflict in Europe was "armed neutrality." But in the interim, he had changed his mind to the position that America must enter the conflict:

> When I addressed the Congress on the 26th of February last, I thought that it would suffice to assert our neutral rights with arms, our right to use the seas against unlawful

interference, our right to keep our people safe against unlawful violence. But armed neutrality, it now appears, is impracticable.[5]

Wilson was arguing very big here by framing the U.S. entry into war in terms of his changed view. Applied to a dinner table discussion on Iraq, this strategy might sound like this:

> In the weeks immediately following September 11, 2001, we all knew that the people who crashed the planes were disciples of Osama Bin Laden in Afghanistan. Back then, I believed that we had a responsibility to respond. But now we are in Iraq, and my position has changed.

This position follows Wilson's by framing the debate in terms of a much bigger picture than just our own personal position. Instead, we are setting the terms for debate right at the beginning of the issue and then moving forward.

What Wilson did next was to define the danger that had changed his view, along with the corresponding action that needed to be taken:

> It is common prudence in such circumstances, grim necessity indeed, to endeavor to destroy them before they have shown their own intention. They must be dealt with upon sight, if dealt with at all.[6]

The similarity between Wilson's view of the German submarines and the current situation in which we find ourselves today is astounding. When we were attacked on September 11th, President Bush at first made a decision to similar to Wilson's case for preemptive strikes against the submarines themselves: since a Bin Laden cell had attacked the United States, we attacked a Bin Laden cell. Like Wilson, Bush initially went after the specific danger we faced. Then, everything changed as Bush decided to expand the conflict beyond attacking Bin Laden's followers before "they had shown their own intention," to attacking a country that had no connection to Bin Laden—a country that was, in fact, an enemy of Bin Laden. Thus, Wilson's speech provides us with the next possible point for arguing big on the war:

> The great danger of continuing to occupy Iraq is not simply that Iraq had absolutely no connection to the Bin Laden followers who attacked us on September 11, and was in fact an enemy of Bin Laden. By staying in Iraq, we have abandoned the work of striking at Bin Laden's followers before his followers can strike at us. And the danger is even greater, because, as we have seen many times since we invaded Iraq, Bin Laden's followers are hidden and active everywhere. And so we must refocus our efforts.

By arguing "big" in this way, the discussion will proceed along progressive lines, raising questions about the urgency of the dangers we face when military resources and attention are poured into Iraq, rather than on the urgent need to find and face Bin Laden's followers. Such a discussion does not simply state a danger and exploit it. (In fact, the entire frame does not mention the word "terrorist" once.) Instead, this new approach argues big, setting the frame for a real debate about real national security. Hopefully, the ascension of Democrats to control of Congress has shown that more Americans are now open to this progressive frame.

7. HAPPINESS IS ACHIEVEMENT

FRANKLIN D. ROOSEVELT, FIRST INAUGURAL ADDRESS (1933)[1]

Keywords: confidence, employment, fear, money, profit, success

Strategy: Health and Happiness—War is "Joining Up"—Creativity versus Money

Quote

"The money changers have fled from their high seats in the temple of our civilization. We may now restore that temple to the ancient truths. The measure of the restoration lies in the extent to which we apply social values more noble than mere monetary profit. Happiness lies not in the mere possession of money; it lies in the joy of achievement, in the thrill of creative effort. The joy and moral stimulation of work no longer must be forgotten in the mad chase of evanescent profits. These dark days will be worth all they cost us if they teach us that our true destiny is not to be ministered unto but to minister to ourselves and to our fellow men. Recognition of the falsity of material wealth as the standard of success goes hand in hand with the abandonment of the false belief that public office and high political position are to be valued only by the standards of pride of place and personal profit; and there must be an end to a conduct in banking and in business which too often has given to a sacred trust the likeness of callous and selfish wrongdoing. Small wonder that confidence languishes, for it thrives only on honesty, on honor, on the sacredness of obligations, on faithful protection, on unselfish performance; without them it cannot live. Restoration calls, however, not for changes in ethics alone. This Nation asks for action, and action now. Our greatest primary task is to put people to work. This is no unsolvable problem if we face it wisely and courageously. It can be accomplished in part by direct recruiting by the Government itself, treating the task as we would treat the emergency of a war, but at the same time, through this employment, accomplishing greatly needed projects to stimulate and reorganize the use of our natural resources. Hand in hand with this we must frankly recognize the overbalance of population in our industrial centers and, by engaging on a national scale in a redistribution, endeavor to provide a better use of the land for those best fitted for the land. The task can be helped by definite efforts to raise the values of agricultural products and with this the power to purchase the output of our cities. It can be helped by preventing realistically the tragedy of the growing loss through foreclosure of our small homes and our farms. It can be helped by insistence that the Federal, State, and local governments act forthwith on the demand that their cost be drastically reduced. It can be helped by the unifying of relief activities which today are often scattered, uneconomical, and unequal. It can be helped by national planning for and supervision of all forms of transportation and of communications and other utilities which have a definitely public character. There are many ways in which it can be helped, but it can never be helped merely by talking about it. We must act and act quickly."

ANALYSIS

When Roosevelt's first inaugural was broadcast over the radio, it carried on a new era started in 1925 by President Calvin Coolidge—an age where it was possible to listen to a presidential speech without being in the audience on the day it was given. As a result, most Americans, both then and now, have actually heard Roosevelt himself say the famous line "We have nothing to fear, but fear itself." While many people today probably think this line came from Roosevelt's December 8, 1941 speech—his address to Congress immediately following the attack on Pearl Harbor—in this earlier speech, Roosevelt was referring not to the "fear" of being attacked by the Japanese, but the "fear" that the U.S. economy would never recover from the Great Depression.[2]

The famous line comes early in the speech, and is memorable because it is so poetic. The real power of Roosevelt's speech, however, was the broad frame he used to define happiness. In Roosevelt's logic [happiness] is [achievement], not just having a lot of money. To the nation that day, Roosevelt said, "Look, we are miserable because we are allowing the wrong people to define what it means for us to be happy." The wrong people were the bankers or, as he called them, the "money changers." As Roosevelt saw it, the bankers had convinced the American people that in order for the nation to thrive again, all citizens needed to do was regain their confidence in the financial markets. "Happiness" in that frame was "faith in the markets." And if one's idea of happiness was tied to the notion of healthy or strong markets, then the logical solution to national economic and social depression was to simply have people regain their faith in the system of lending. But it was not that simple, as poverty was clearly not the result of the American people's failure to believe in the markets.

Today, Americans can understand the kind of logic that Roosevelt was arguing against because contemporary Republicans are constantly trying to convince us that our happiness depends entirely on our faith in free markets. And, therein, lay the true genius of Roosevelt's speech: rather than proposing ways to restore market confidence, Roosevelt moved the discussion to an entirely new frame, by redefining the very idea of happiness:

> Happiness lies not in the mere possession of money; it lies in the joy of achievement, in the thrill of creative effort.

The joy and moral stimulation of work no longer must be forgotten in the mad chase of evanescent profits. These dark days will be worth all they cost us if they teach us that our true destiny is not to be ministered unto but to minister to ourselves and to our fellow men.

This passage about "happiness" deserves much more recognition in our list of presidential greatest hits than Roosevelt's line about "fear itself." Why? Because in this section of the speech, Roosevelt liberated the nation from the shackles that had confined the American sense of purpose and progress. It was a transformation that changed this nation for the better—forever.

In the next part of the speech, Roosevelt elaborated on the frame he had set up, turning from the logic of [happiness] to the meaning of personal and political [success]:

Recognition of the falsity of material wealth as the standard of success goes hand in hand with the abandonment of the false belief that public office and high political position are to be valued only by the standards of pride of place and personal profit.[3]

Roosevelt's goal was not to define "material wealth," but to realign it with a new moral conclusion: wealth itself is not success, cannot restore national confidence, and is not the essential building block of the American dream. By reframing [happiness], Roosevelt reconnected the American people with the most basic of constitutional principles: life, liberty, and the pursuit of happiness. If ever there was a speech that refuted the basic principles of "trickle down" economics, it was Roosevelt's first inaugural address.

Having reframed the nature of the problem the country faced, Roosevelt then set about reframing how the nation should go about solving its immense domestic problems. In policy terms, what Roosevelt proposed in his speech was a wholesale turning inward of

American social and economic concerns: he wanted to break away from global concerns in the short run in order to restore dignity to a downtrodden nation. His policies under the New Deal would constitute a spectacular investment in public works coupled with a massive hiring of private citizens. The end goal was to lift the spirits of the American people, modernize the American landscape, and jumpstart the American economy.

To frame this project, Roosevelt declared war, albeit not in any conventional sense:

> Our greatest primary task is to put people to work. This is no unsolvable problem if we face it wisely and courageously. It can be accomplished in part by direct recruiting by the Government itself, treating the task as we would treat the emergency of a war, but at the same time, through this employment, accomplishing greatly needed projects to stimulate and reorganize the use of our natural resources.[4]

It is difficult to overstate how remarkable the concept that Roosevelt proposed was. The very idea that the restoration of America would be based on the government stepping up and putting people to work was revolutionary. A government dedicated to protecting the people's rights to life and liberty would become under Roosevelt's proposals a government that hired the unemployed for public works projects. The policy, to many, would look like socialism. But by framing the task of solving unemployment as an "emergency of war," Roosevelt successfully argued that the solution to the Great Depression lay in mass mobilization of the public.

Roosevelt's frame of confronting national social crises with the "emergency of war" is radically different than the contemporary cliché that the nation must fight a "war on" this or that. For Roosevelt, talking about a solution to a problem as "war" was not a prelude to justifying state-sponsored violence or killing, but a strategy for inspiring every citizen to enlist in a social contract. Facing the Great Depression with the "emergency of war" required participation from every citizen. Once Roosevelt framed poverty and crisis in these terms, those elements in government and industry who reserved participation for the privileged or powerful were identified as enemies of progress. In Roosevelt's frame, where achievement was the key to happiness, the currency of national restoration was participation. It is no wonder that the great innovations of Roosevelt's presidency remain the solid foundation of a confident and lasting American democracy.

Roosevelt's First Inaugural Address presents rich possibilities for framing in the contemporary progressive movement. His framing of happiness and achievement can serve as a role model for progressive politicians, activists, and citizens seeking to lead the debate on the seemingly insurmountable problems of our day. To see where Roosevelt can be used today, progressives need only to ask, "What is the Great Depression of our day?" Thinking in those terms is a way of thinking big—of focusing attention on our seemingly insurmountable problems, and then solving them.

STRATEGY

[Politician]—Health and Happiness

Perhaps the greatest potential for applying Roosevelt's framing is with the current crisis in America's healthcare system—an emergency of the same order as the economic depression of the 1930s. In times of unprecedented wealth and prosperity, tens of millions of Americans live without the resources to access basic medical care. And similar to what Roosevelt said about the Great Depression, we are unable to surmount the healthcare crisis because the "money changers" have seized hold of the "temple of civilization."

Roosevelt understood that to escape the Great Depression, Americans needed to stop trying to fix the banks and instead take actions to restore confidence of individuals. Similarly, the solution to America's current healthcare "depression" is to stop trying to fix the insurance industry and instead take actions to restore the health of individuals. That way, the achievement of good health amongst individual citizens can become the engine that drives reform in our healthcare system.

The frame? Good health starts with people, not money. For a candidate or elected official giving a policy speech on this topic, one way to drive the debate toward a progressive vision would be to steal a page directly from Roosevelt's reframing of "happiness." In the following passages, I have lifted the phrasing directly from Roosevelt's speech and swapped the concept of "happiness" with concepts related to "good health." The result presents a whole range of possibilities for a contemporary progressive speech:

- Restoring our nation to good health lies in the extent to which we apply social values more noble than mere monetary profit.
- Good health must never depend on the possession of money; it must instead lie in the joy of community and in the thrill of caring for others.
- The moral stimulation of good health must no longer be forgotten in the mad chase for profits.
- Recognition of the falsity of material wealth as the standard of good health goes hand in hand with the abandonment of the false belief that public office and high political position are to be valued only by the standards of personal profit.
- Restoration calls not for changes in ethics alone. This Nation calls for action, and action now.

The secret is not to just cut and paste Roosevelt's words into the current debate, but to rediscover the power of his framing. Progressive solutions to healthcare cannot simply take the form of coverage proposals and statistical analyses revealing insurance company revenues. While these policy details matter in the long-term, initially it is the framing that sets the tone of the discussion. Before progressives can lead the national debate on restoring America's healthcare system, the concept of "health" itself must be reframed away from its current economic-based concepts and towards a frame of [good health] as [people] and [caring].

[Activist]—War Is "Joining Up"

One of the biggest questions on the mind of any progressive activist is "how do I frame what I say to inspire people to participate?" For activists, the biggest framing lesson in Roosevelt's first inaugural speech has nothing to with "fear" or "happiness" or "restoration," but with his use of the "war" metaphor.

Activism is often thankless work, requiring the hard work of countless nameless, faceless "boots on the ground." In addition, activists are rarely thanked for their efforts, rarely paid, and typically forgotten. But without activists, progressive goals would never get off the ground. The challenge for any activist group, is to find ways to appeal to new recruits despite the less than obvious rewards of the work.

Roosevelt's speech suggests a great solution by reminding us that when we use "war" as a metaphor in political debate, we do so to inspire people to join the social cause of the progressive movement, not as a pretext for talking about the violence we wish to wage on this or that social ill. When President Bush talks about the "War on Terror," for example, he always talks about "killing" the "killers." For Republicans, the war frame is an excuse to ratchet up the rhetoric in order to talk about violence. They have corrupted this important progressive frame, and activists must take it back.

To remember what the war metaphor really means when used in politics, it might be helpful to recall an image that most Americans are familiar with: James Flagg's 1916 U.S. Army recruiting poster featuring Uncle Sam dressed in top hat and pointing his finger, with the caption "I Want YOU For U.S. Army."[5] The message of that famous poster is the same message that Roosevelt invoked when he talked about "treating the task as we would treat the emergency of a war." In these instances, "war" is not a call to violence, but a metaphor for the "emergency" need for people to participate.

To frame an issue with this progressive war frame, activists can use words that evoke "emergency" and "recruitment," rather than the words of violence and death. For example, when sending an email to a list of potential volunteers for an election campaign, the team leader might write something along these lines:

- I WANT YOU FOR CAMPAIGN VOLUNTEER
- Don't Wait—PARTICIPATE!
- Urgent need for boots on the ground this weekend:
  phone banking
  district walking
  visibility duty
  polling monitors
- Join the last minute emergency recruits. We need what you have. Join up and help elect a progressive candidate today!

The key to this frame is a true understanding of what Roosevelt was saying in his speech: that the power of mobilizing people for a war effort resides in the ability of a leader to inspire people to service, not to violence. When used to frame the debate, "war" builds a logic of involvement couched in a history of defending American principles in times of great need.

[Citizen]—Creativity versus Money

The debate with a conservative about corporations yields a frustration that every progressive has experienced. The situation is familiar: You are sitting at the dinner table and the topic of teenage obesity comes up. Your conservative cousin says, "If people are stupid enough to eat that horrible food, they deserve to be fat!" To which you respond, "It's the fault of the corporations, they are just in it to make money." Both of these arguments lead to nothing but frustration. What is wrong with the progressive argument that faults corporations with focusing too much on making money?

Actually, money is not really the big criticism that progressives have with large corporations. Our real concern, as Roosevelt points out, is the tendency for large corporations to sap creativity and vision when they are put in charge of large sectors of American life. The problem is not that corporations make a profit, but that they stop using that profit to energize and strengthen the principles that sustain American life. Corporations quickly become "faced with failure," to use Roosevelt's phrase, and thus it is the job of progressives to refocus attention on what is important.

Roosevelt's speech suggests that if progressives frame their arguments about corporations in terms of "creativity," then the smaller point about profit will fall into place much more easily. Consider this example of how the conversation about teenage obesity might unfold if following this strategy:

> The problem is not that people make bad choices, but that the larger and wealthier a corporation like McDonalds becomes, the less creativity it puts into its food. With the profits that McDonalds earns, they should be able to single handedly drive even the most overweight American toward a healthier diet. But their creativity vanishes the bigger they get. We all know this to be true. A great restaurant starts off small, with good food. Suddenly, they get successful, open a few franchises and before you know it, the food turns into junk. Teaching people to make better choices is important. But corporations that lack the creativity to produce healthy food that also tastes good is a much larger part of the problem.

The conversation can now unfold with a strong criticism of corporate practice without getting bogged down in the un-winnable attack on corporate profit. By framing the debate in terms of the corporate failure of creativity, the conversation will now head toward how to motivate and invigorate corporate practice to be more in line with broad national goals.

The point about the corporate failure of creativity may seem like a small point in Roosevelt's speech, but it has the potential to completely transform how progressives approach debate on a host of topics tied to corporate practice.

8. US AGAINST THEM

HARRY TRUMAN, INAUGURAL ADDRESS (1949)[1]

Keywords: belief, enemy, faith, opposition, orientation, threat

Strategy: Get Oriented—Strong and Fast—Burning Building

Quote

"The peoples of the earth face the future with great uncertainty, composed equally of great hopes and great fears . . . It is fitting, therefore, that we take this occasion to proclaim to the world the essential principles of the faith by which we live, and to declare our aims to all peoples.

The American people stand firm in the faith which has inspired this Nation from the beginning. We believe that all men have a right to equal justice under law and equal opportunity to share in the common good. We believe that all men have a right to freedom of thought and expression. We believe that all men are created equal because they are created in the image of God. From this faith we will not be moved. The American people desire, and are determined to work for, a world in which all nations and all peoples are free to govern themselves as they see fit, and to achieve a decent and satisfying life. Above all else, our people desire, and are determined to work for, peace on earth—a just and lasting peace—based on genuine agreement freely arrived at by equals.

In the pursuit of these aims, the United States and other like-minded nations find themselves directly opposed by a regime with contrary aims and a totally different concept of life. That regime adheres to a false philosophy which purports to offer freedom, security, and greater opportunity to mankind. Misled by that philosophy, many peoples have sacrificed their liberties only to learn to their sorrow that deceit and mockery, poverty and tyranny, are their reward. That false philosophy is communism.

Communism is based on the belief that man is so weak and inadequate that he is unable to govern himself, and therefore requires the rule of strong masters. Democracy is based on the conviction that man has the moral and intellectual capacity, as well as the inalienable right, to govern himself with reason and justice. Communism subjects the individual to arrest without lawful cause, punishment without trial, and forced labor as the chattel of the state. It decrees what information he shall receive, what art he shall produce, what leaders he shall follow, and what thoughts he shall think. Democracy maintains that government is established for the benefit of the individual, and is charged with the responsibility of protecting the rights of the individual and his freedom in the exercise of those abilities of his. Communism maintains that social wrongs can be corrected only by violence. Democracy has proved that social justice can be achieved through peaceful change. Communism holds that the world is so widely divided into opposing classes that war is inevitable. Democracy holds that free nations can settle differences justly and maintain a lasting peace.

These differences between communism and democracy do not concern the United States alone. People everywhere are coming to realize that what is involved is material well-being, human dignity, and the right to believe in and worship God. I state these differences, not to draw issues of belief as such, but because the actions resulting from the Communist philosophy are a threat to the efforts of free nations to bring about world recovery and lasting peace."

ANALYSIS

One of the more remarkable moments in the history of presidential framing, Harry Truman's inaugural speech—delivered just months after the Soviet Union had tested its first nuclear bomb—did no less than divide the entire world into two opposing camps: us and them. As such, it remains one of the signature statements of the Cold War.[2]

Since September 11, 2001, a similar strategy of framing foreign affairs in terms of two diametrically opposed positions has been exploited by President Bush and the Republican Party to advance military aggression in Iraq, breach foreign treaties, and conduct illegal electronic spying at home.[3] While the circumstances that surrounded Truman were different than in contemporary America, his 1949 Inaugural Speech is one of the best case studies for understanding how and why the "enemy" frame works.

Looking closely at Truman's inaugural speech, we might be inclined to believe that the frame's power comes entirely through the depiction of the enemy—in his case, communism. In fact, the depiction of the enemy is only one of three elements that make up the "enemy" frame, which are: principle, orientation and enemy, and are combined as follows:

[principle] < orientation > [enemy]

When sketched out as a simple formula, we begin to see how the "enemy" frame can control a debate: once we hear that two forces are oriented against one another, we must make a choice: us or them? Truman's inaugural address was a powerful speech, in other words, not just because he declared communism a "false philosophy," but because he framed communism using the "enemy" formula.

To do this, Truman first defined the "essential principles" which Americans upheld, presenting a list of three statements of "faith" that had "inspired the Nation" from its onset:

- We believe that all men have a right to equal justice under the law and equal opportunity to share in the common good.
- We believe that all men have a right to freedom of thought and expression.
- We believe that all men are created equal because they are created in the image of God.[4]

Taken as a whole, Truman's "we believe" statements were reinterpretations of the Constitution's "life, liberty and the pursuit of happiness," albeit restated in terms contemporary to 1949. Accordingly, by defining the principles that Americans held on faith, Truman put in place the first element of the frame:

[American democracy] < orientation > [enemy]

Next, Truman invoked a metaphor that placed the American faith in democracy in opposition to another "faith":

In the pursuit of these aims, the United States and other like-minded nations find themselves directly opposed by a regime with contrary aims and a totally different concept of life.[5]

In this passage the word "opposed" invokes a metaphor that describes the American faith in democracy as if it were a person—or even an army—standing directly opposite another "regime with contrary aims." Truman's use of the word "opposed" did more than just explain; it called up a spatial logic in the minds of his listener. American faith in democracy, thus, became a real thing in the speech, not just an abstract statement of principle.

Having defined his opening principle and orientated it with a metaphor, two elements of Truman's frame were in place:

[American democracy] < opposed by > [enemy]

The remaining piece of Truman's frame was the enemy: communism. In the speech, communism was depicted not just as something bad, but as the exact opposite of American "faith" in democracy, a "false philosophy." Thus, Truman described communism as dismissive of the inherent rights of individuals through the force of "strong masters," "forced labor," and an all powerful, all imposing state.

To drive home this point of communism as the enemy of American democracy, Truman unleashed a series of contrasting statements pitting the principles of democracy against the anti-principles of communism's false philosophy. In each case, what communism proposed was the exact opposite of what the American people held dear, thereby putting in place the third element of the "enemy" frame:

[American democracy] < opposed by > [communism]

After listening to Truman's powerful framing of communism as an enemy that opposed the American system of belief and governance, it would have been virtually impossible for even an expert in presidential rhetoric to not be persuaded. Not even Truman's harshest critics could have thought, "Wait a second, here . . . communism can't be an 'enemy.' Ideas are not armies . . . this is just a metaphor . . . our real enemy is Stalinist Russia . . . Truman is framing this debate to persuade me to support his new policies!"

What Truman's speech allows us to see is that the "enemy" frame persuades the listener not simply by naming an enemy: It frames that enemy in opposition to ourselves through strategic use of principles, orientational metaphors, and repetition. And in this structure, we see a core frame that defined not just communism in the minds of Truman's audience that day in 1949, but a frame that held sway over the entire nation for the duration of the Cold War.

A half-century after Truman's inaugural address, President George W. Bush would invoke the "enemy" frame in his famous "Axis of Evil" State of the Union Address—the speech that framed the "War on Terror."[6] In that speech, delivered to a nation still in shock following the attacks of September 11, 2001, President Bush claimed that anyone—nation or otherwise—who did not support his foreign policy decisions was tantamount to a terrorist sympathizer and would be treated as an enemy. Bush's speech shows the potential for abuse of the "enemy" frame by ideologically driven leaders. Unlike Truman, Bush used the "enemy" frame not simply to define the national security concerns of the new century, but as an aggressive tactic for undermining his political opponents. Indeed, while the "enemy" frame is used to persuade the public of the impending threat of a new danger, it is also used to obscure, to over-simplify, and—most problematically of all—to trap and smear the other side in a political campaign. Nowhere was this tactic more apparent than in the final days of the 2006 midterm elections when the President gave a series stump speeches defining a vote for the Democratic Party as a vote for the enemy.[7]

Reframing the "War on Terror" is not just a pressing concern of progressives in America—it is the essential political challenge of this generation. Since September 11, 2001, Republicans under the leadership of President Bush and Vice President Cheney have spent billions of dollars framing the "War on Terror" in terms of an America dedicated to "freedom" in opposition to "terrorism." How can politicians, activists and citizens re-frame the "War on Terror" such that Americans would think through the security threats that we face as a nation through a different logic? The answer is to use our understanding of the "enemy" frame from Truman's inaugural speech to (1) re-orient the metaphor, (2) name the principle, and (3) claim the threat we face.

STRATEGY

[Politician] - Get Oriented

One of the key lessons from Truman's inaugural address is that political debates can be controlled by repeating a metaphor: in particular, metaphors that orient. If President Bush repeats over and over again that our national security depends on us "opposing" the terrorists, then it becomes more and more difficult to think outside that box. The solution, then, is to re-orient the debate.

Instead of framing national security in terms that trap us in the logic of "opposition to" an enemy, progressives might say the following:

- The United States must stay **in front** of groups that seek to harm us
- Our policy is to **contain** potential threats.
- America must stand **beside** its allies
- The nation is secure when we stay **on top of** every threat
- Terrorism will threaten us so long as we are always **two steps behind** Al Qaeda

In front, contain, beside, on top, two steps behind—these are all metaphors that orient the public towards a more progressive view of national security, an approach based on principles of cooperation and protection, not confrontation and aggression.

For example, if a candidate is asked how she would deal with the threat of terrorism, she might orient the debate by saying:

Keeping America trapped in a head-to-head struggle with no possible exit is exactly what small groups that use terror want. They wish to be made legitimate forces by drawing the big kid on the block into a head-to-head fight, and the longer we give in to them, the more uncertain and unsafe our future will be. What threatens us is not just terrorism, but our own lack of creativity, our own lack of speed, our own failure to stay in front. To secure the nation against terrorist groups, the United States military must stay ahead of those who seek to harm us. And we must do so not by sheer force of collision, but by standing beside our allies and partners, by acting faster and smarter at every turn.

Progressives will not be able to control the debate on national security until they frame the debate to show that a rash, blind tactic of head on collision makes things worse. The war and occupation in Iraq, in other words, are not just bad strategies for catching the terrorists: those tactics are the products of a fundamentally flawed understanding of national security that comes through a misuse of the "enemy" frame.

[Activist]—Strong and Fast

To be effective in reframing, progressive activists should try whenever possible to use progressive terms for the particular debate in question. On national security, the phrase that Republicans initiated and have used since September 11, 2001 is "War on Terror." How can progressive activists move beyond this phrase?

To get out of the "'War on Terror," activists need to shift to a new frame. Truman's speech helps us see that the "War on Terror" is fundamentally an extension of the logic invoked by the "enemy" frame. When we say "War on Terror" we are really repeating an abbreviated version of this rather awkward construction:

> Americans with a faith in Democracy are engaged in a war
> in opposition to radical groups seeking to undermine and
> destroy that Democracy.

When stated in its entirely, we can see that the full phrase behind "War on Terror" is very similar to the frame we saw in Truman's Inaugural Address:

> [Americans] < opposed to > [communism]
> [Americans] < opposed to > [terrorism]

Although Truman never used the phrase "War on Communism," the frame is the same as we find in "war on terror." We just need to swap out "communism" for "terrorism" and the structure of the argument is right there.

At this point in the process of reframing national security, progressive activists should remind themselves that, of course, they are opposed to terrorism. The purpose of changing the frame is precisely because progressives are concerned about protecting the nation, and recognize deep problems in the current approach. But unless we dislodge the phrase "War on Terror," progressive activists will continue to reinforce a frame of terrorism that leaves us locked in a destructive and ineffective vision of national security.

So, walk over to a new frame. For example, the next time a progressive activist is phone banking for a candidate, they can explain the candidate's national security position in terms of this frame:

Smart Security

To say that security is "smart" is to use a metaphor that looks like this:

[national security] is [an intelligent person]

Aside from obvious critiques of the current Republican administration that flows effortlessly from this frame, the following general script can quickly sketch out what is meant by "smart security" during a phone call to a potential voter:

- We protect America best with **smart security**.
- To be safe, we must **find, analyze and understand** threats before they get to us.
- We must **anticipate** moves ahead of our enemies.
- In the 21st Century, national defense must constantly **innovate.**
- Our efforts to work with our allies must be as **path breaking** as the technology we **invent** to defend against the dangers of the future.

These terms (in bold) invoke the "smart security" frame and establish an entirely new logic. In a conversation that frames the candidate's position on national security in this way, an activist can engage a voter in discussion of new defense technology, strategies for gathering intelligence, and tactics for maintaining international cooperation. But, more importantly, the "smart security" frame liberates the national security debate from the phrase "War on Terror," thereby allowing the activist to advance a progressive vision of a stronger, safer nation.

[Citizen]—Burning Building

Progressives always dread the dinner table conversation about Iraq because it inevitably ends with somebody saying, "Democrats just want to cut and run—we need to fight them over there, or else they'll attack us over here!" If we know this logic is wrong, why then is the "fight them over there" logic so effective? The answer lies in the dynamic of the "enemy" frame.

As Truman's speech taught us, the "enemy" frame defines national security in terms of strict oppositional forces: us against. them. It dictates that safety is the product of one set of principles locked in head-to-head opposition with an enemy that embodies the antithesis of everything we seek to protect. It is principle pushing against anti-principle—like two giant ideological linebackers grappling against one another. In this logic, the "fight them over there" logic is not just about strategy, but invokes a metaphor of America's military as a defensive line. When progressives propose a change in military policy, Republicans accuse them of wanting to suddenly stop playing defense, thereby allowing the "evil" other team to thunder down field unopposed.

To counter "fight them over there," progressives must do more than just say, "No we won't!" We need to move the discussion to a new metaphor about America's military where "fight them over there" can be understood in certain instances as the most dangerous option. One possibility is a fire brigade metaphor:

[America's military] is [a fire brigade]

In this logic, our military is not locked in a head to head struggle against an enemy, but instead is a smart and fast force that responds to "fires" and puts them out. The most dangerous scenario for such a force is a "burning building," where the goal is to rush into the building based on a plan to rescue those in danger, to contain the damage of the fire as much as possible, and then leave. In this logic, the worst possible decision any fire brigade can make is to enter a burning building and then—because the fire was still burning—to stay inside.

The logic of the "burning building" may seem abstract at first, but when the subject of Iraq comes up in a dinner table conversation, it might be used along the following lines:

- Iraq has burst into flames
- We should not trap our troops inside Iraq as it burns.
- We must change our policy before the roof collapses in flames on our soldiers.
- If we don't act soon, we will need a five-alarm rescue to save our soldiers.

The goal need not be to lay out a clear military policy, but to establish the terms of the debate. Using this new frame, if someone at the table says, "We need to fight them over there!" an effective answer might be:

It's not about fighting over there or over here, but about pulling out of the building before it collapses and kills everyone. Then we can regroup, retool, and get back to work. But if we just drop to our knees in fear of actually walking out of the burning building, then we doom ourselves and our most idealistic and dedicated young Americans to a horrible, yet easily avoided, disaster.

As you can see, once the "burning building" frame has been set, the "fight them over there" argument is no longer an effective debate maneuver. The end result will be a real conversation about the urgent need to retool America's policies in Iraq—and everywhere else—in a way that is fast, smart, and responsive to the actual dangers we face on the ground.

9. BALANCE IN PROGRESS

DWIGHT EISENHOWER, FAREWELL ADDRESS (1961)[1]

Keywords: corporations, diplomacy, defense, research, judgment

Strategy: Corruption as Imbalance—The Front Door—
Dinner Table Generals

Quote

"Crises there will continue to be. In meeting them, whether foreign or domestic, great or small, there is a recurring temptation to feel that some spectacular and costly action could become the miraculous solution to all current difficulties. A huge increase in newer elements of our defense; development of unrealistic programs to cure every ill in agriculture; a dramatic expansion in basic and applied research—these and many other possibilities, each possibly promising in itself, may be suggested as the only way to the road we wish to travel. But each proposal must be weighed in the light of a broader consideration: the need to maintain balance in and among national programs-balance between the private and the public economy, balance between cost and hoped for advantage—balance between the clearly necessary and the comfortably desirable; balance between our essential requirements as a nation and the duties imposed by the nation upon the individual; balance between actions of the moment and the national welfare of the future. Good judgment seeks balance and progress; lack of it eventually finds imbalance and frustration. The record of many decades stands as proof that our people and their government have, in the main, understood these truths and have responded to them well, in the face of stress and threat. But threats, new in kind or degree, constantly arise. I mention two only. A vital element in keeping the peace is our military establishment. Our arms must be mighty, ready for instant action, so that no potential aggressor may be tempted to risk his own destruction. Our military organization today bears little relation to that known by any of my predecessors in peacetime, or indeed by the fighting men of World War II or Korea. Until the latest of our world conflicts, the United States had no armaments industry. American makers of plowshares could, with time and as required, make swords as well. But now we can no longer risk emergency improvisation of national defense; we have been compelled to create a permanent armaments industry of vast proportions. Added to this, three and a half million men and women are directly engaged in the defense establishment. We annually spend on military security more than the net income of all United States corporations. This conjunction of an immense military establishment and a large arms industry is new in the American experience. The total influence-economic, political, even spiritual—is felt in every city, every State house, every office of the Federal government. We recognize the imperative need for this development. Yet we must not fail to comprehend its grave implications. Our toil, resources and livelihood are all involved; so is the very structure of our society. In the councils of government, we must guard against the acquisition of unwarranted influence, whether sought or unsought, by the military-industrial complex. The potential for the disastrous rise of misplaced power exists and will persist. We must never let the weight of this combination endanger our liberties or democratic processes. We should take nothing for granted. Only an alert and knowledgeable citizenry can compel the proper meshing of the huge industrial and military machinery of defense with our peaceful methods and goals, so that security and liberty may prosper together."

ANALYSIS

There are few speeches in history more germane to contemporary progressive politics than President Dwight Eisenhower's 1961 Farewell Address. In almost every aspect, it was a prophetic speech when it was delivered, and it has continued to stand as a moral and civic blueprint of the problems we face, as well as showing the path to solutions.

Delivered just before the end of his second term, Eisenhower's speech addressed the rising threat of new and powerful forces in American society that, if not addressed, had the potential to derail the moral and civic foundation of the United States. The great threat that Eisenhower foresaw was that the United States would lose "balance" as military, financial and scientific forces gained a new foothold on the imagination and policies of the federal government.

What is this "balance" that he spoke about? In simplest terms, "balance" can be seen as an equation or a set of scales with equal measures or values on both sides. When the cost, weight or value of one side [x] equals the cost, weight or value of the other side [y] then the result is "balanced" as follows:

$$[x] = [y]$$

When we read Eisenhower's farewell speech, we get a glimpse into the mind of a leader who thought in terms of equal measure, equal force, and equal influence as the key to maintaining good judgment and good government. Among the things that Eisenhower insisted should remained "balanced" were:

Private economy	=	Public economy
Cost of advantage	=	Hoped for advantage
Clearly necessary	=	Comfortably desirable
Essential requirements	=	Duties imposed
Actions of the moment	=	Welfare of the Future

However, Eisenhower saw new forces emerging in America that threatened to push government out of balance, like a scale where one side is too heavy and pushes the other side to the ground.

To demonstrate what he meant, he drew on three specific examples: (1) the rise of corporations dedicated to supplying the country with ready weapons for the Cold War; (2) the growing influence of government money in scientific research, and scientific research in government policy; (3) the rise of deficit spending. These three factors, according to Eisenhower, had the potential to cloud the judgment of America's leaders, which would result in catastrophic decisions.

How prophetic Eisenhower was. It is almost as if his speech foresaw the Vietnam War and the invasion of Iraq, people like Robert McNamara and Donald Rumsfeld, the rise of corporations like Halliburton, and the massive overspending of the administrations of Ronald Reagan and George W. Bush.

However, in looking closely at Eisenhower's speech, it is important to distinguish between the phrase and the frame. Consider this passage, for example, where Eisenhower uttered what has become his most famous sound bite (emphasis added):

> In the councils of government, we must guard against the acquisition of unwarranted influence, whether sought or unsought, by **the military-industrial complex**. The potential for the disastrous rise of misplaced power exists and will persist.

What a powerful progressive frame—spoken by a Republican! But the power in this part of the speech is not the "military-industrial complex" phrase, but the way Eisenhower frames it through the logic of "balance."

Just prior to the phrase, Eisenhower had explained that the conditions by which the United States prepared for war had changed dramatically. Previously, when the president declared war, the national economy would, over a period of time, switch into war mode in order to create the people (troops) and materials necessary to fight. During the Cold War, however, when the country was constantly under threat of a war that could be launched and underway in a matter of minutes, the need to have equipment and people always at the ready had created whole industries whose purpose was to always be prepared for war—industries whose wealth was greater than all other U.S. industries combined. Eisenhower felt that the dominant presence of these war-related industries created an imbalance that weighed down the judgment of those in government.

Indeed, the metaphor of "balance" is infused throughout Eisenhower's statements about the military industry. He talks in terms of the "rise" of power and the military's massive financial, industrial and human capital. While all these resources could have been described as contributing to the readiness of the nation's forces, Eisenhower presented them instead as a massive imbalance, a danger weighing on the nation, tilting America towards the excesses of imperialism.[2]

And, it wasn't just the military-related industries that knocked things out of balance. At another point in the speech, Eisenhower talks about the rise of an irrational exuberance in the field of scientific research—reflecting the early 1960s belief that science could provide singular answers to all our problems. Here, too, Eisenhower emphasized the "balance" frame, warning the American public that good judgment resulted only when options were "weighed" one against another—invoking the classic image of the scales of judgment as the key to sound government.

Eisenhower literally saw the threat of imbalance in almost every corner of American society as it headed into the 1960s, filling his speech with myriad examples of areas that were in danger of future crisis due to a loss of balance, such as:

Academia: too much focus on government grants, not enough on ideas

Diplomacy: too much emphasis on military solutions, not enough effort to bring weaker nations to the negotiating table

Spending: too much spent on short-term gain, not enough planning for long-term solvency

Industry: too much investment in massive industry, not enough in small business

Productivity: too much investment in technology, not enough in people

Statesmanship: too much emphasis on casting out old ideas, not enough on integrating old with new

Public Policy: too much emphasis on a scientific-technological elite, not enough on seasoned policy makers

As these examples show, the power of Eisenhower's "balance" frame remains relevant today, and not just because the dangers he warned us about nearly fifty years ago are still present. Rather, the frame still works because it is the clearest, most direct logic to invoke when a President seeks to warn the public about the threat that extremes present to the decision making process at the heart of government.

Encoded deep in the American psyche is the idea that our government was set up in "balance" by the framers of the Constitution, a balance between three branches of government, each preventing the other from imposing their will unjustly on the other. In addition, our country also operates on a balance between the interests of the states and the interests of the whole. We understand these things from a very early age, when we are first introduced to the principles of independence and liberty that anchor our national narrative.

Eisenhower's farewell speech did not reinvent the "balance" frame so much as ground it in a new set of pressing concerns. The extent to which we still live with those concerns speaks volumes about the value of Eisenhower's language and logic for progressives today. Framing such abstract ideas as "good judgment" or "statesmanship" is an essential task that progressives too often overlook in favor of policy talk. Without a frame for the broad concepts that define how government is supposed to work, progressive policy proposals can appear to be "grasping at straws" to gain support from the public, instead of pushing real policy substance. Eisenhower's farewell address offers a useful and timely model for progressives seeking to frame these broad concepts effectively.

STRATEGY

[Politician]—Corruption as Imbalance

To be more persuasive when making speeches, elected progressive politicians or candidates for office must not only talk about specific laws and policies, but also define what it means for government to be good, sound, and effective. The difference is between a progressive who speaks like a committee member and a progressive who speaks like a leader.

Nowhere is this more important than in the national debate about corruption in our state and federal governments. During the infamous Jack Abramoff "K-Street Project" scandal, we discovered that a key Republican advisor with close ties to the Republican President and Republican leaders of Congress had used private money to wield influence in government. During the lead up to the invasion and occupation of the Iraq war, we discovered that a single corporation on whose board the Republican Vice President sat, and whose stock he still owns (Halliburton), was given no-bid contracts by the Republican government, resulting in massive profiteering from the invasion and occupation of Iraq.[4]

In addressing these issues, progressive politicians choose most often to talk about "oversight" or the "money" or "corruption." These are tremendously important topics. But to be effective in convincing people, they must be framed in terms of a broader definition of "good government." Leading up to the 2006 midterm elections, for example, Congresswoman Nancy Pelosi (D-CA), framed her commitment to changing lobbying rules in the House of Representatives as a desire to "drain the swamp."[5] Pelosi's colorful metaphor was the perfect alternative to technical talk about House rules and procedures. An effective framing strategy, "drain the swamp" helped focus the public's attention beyond individual acts of corruption to a larger, systemic problem created while the government was controlled entirely by Republicans. As such, it turned out to be one of the keys to the Democratic Party's success at regaining a majority in Congress.

Eisenhower's "balance" frame and his use of the word "crisis" provide another good approach to framing corruption. For example, in a discussion about revelations in the Abramoff scandal, Halliburton war profiteering or a similar Republican scandal, a progressive candidate running for office could say:

> Corruption among those who govern is not just a crime by those who commit the crimes, but a crisis of government itself. This is because the very basis of government is good judgment, which can only be maintained if government maintains a balance between public and private interests. When individuals, either for themselves or on behalf of in-dustry, are allowed to purchase and build up influence with elected officials, judgment itself falls off balance. And with-out balance, the foundation of good government collapses. To restore good government we must do more than charge the guilty with their crimes—we must restore the balance that is the basis of good judgment. We must restore our ability to weigh together all the interests of the people.

The "balance" frame provides more than just a moral compass or a definition of principle: it offers a structuring logic that takes the most abstract concepts of all—"good" and "bad"—and defines them through a basic metaphor of evenness and fairness. Ultimately, what is "good" in the minds of most Americans is what is "fair." The willingness of the progressive politician to frame corruption scandals in terms of these broad ideas will be a decisive factor in leading the efforts to clean up the mess.

[Activist]—The Front Door

One of the most fundamental concerns of all progressive activists— particularly in an election season—is getting out the vote, or "GOTV" as it is called in activist circles. We can talk progressive framing all we want, but we cannot truly move closer to a progressive vision unless real people actually show up at the polls on election day and vote for progressive candidates.

How do we get our ideas across to people when we actually find ourselves standing in front of them? The doorbell rings, a potential voter answers, and there we are—notepad in hand—rehearsed script in our heads, ready to give our pitch.

To the great credit of progressives, our first instinct is to talk to voters about issues and policies. While this will always be important, the presentation of issues does not necessarily go hand-in-hand with a "front door" encounter. Issues are best presented on a website where people can "click" and explore, read at their own pace, and search for more information. At the front door, we have to tell our own story, to share our own experience as progressives. While progressive activists are often too modest see it, when standing face to face with a potential new voter, our greatest asset is our own story.

An important framing lesson from Eisenhower's farewell address can help us see how to have great success with the "front door" GOTV encounter. The key is to see that Eisenhower frames good government in terms of "balance." Without balance, good judgment tips towards the interests of the "stronger" factor. No matter how a potential voter may stand on a host of specific progressive issues, they will usually agree that their participation is essential for maintaining the balance of good government. The key is to make sure we tell them this.

And so the next time we find ourselves going door-to-door in a GOTV effort for a campaign or a policy, we might begin by invoking Eisenhower's notion of balance:

> Thanks so much for taking a few minutes to talk with me. I'm here to tell you about [important issue, candidate, etc.], but before I do that I just wanted to share a few thoughts with you about why I volunteer to talk with voters. More and more these days, I believe that balance is the key to good government, and balance means all of us participating. I am here because I believe in [important issue, candidate, etc.], but even more than that, I'm here because I believe our good government depends on my participation and on your participation—it depends on all of us participating. If we do not participate, then our system is out of balance. By not participating we leave our system to just a few. If they make decisions that we do not support, it's not just because they have bad judgment, but because we stayed home—we did not make ourselves part of the process. Even before we talk about [important issue, candidate, etc.]—and I have some great resources to share with you about that—I wanted to start out by talking to you about the role you can play just by showing up, by participating, by making sure that our system keeps its balance and therefore its good judgment.

Of course, some of us are more comfortable with this kind of script than others. But the strategy here is fairly straight-forward: before launching into a discussion of a particular issue or candidate, door-to-door GOTV activists should frame their conversation in terms of the principle of balance in good government. There is no need to invoke President Eisenhower by name, but simply to focus on a very personal and honest statement of what we believe. When we begin our door-to-door presentations this way, we offer a bit of ourselves to our listener, thereby inviting them to reciprocate.

The risk we take, of course, is that the person at the door may simply say "I know this already!" and shut the door in our face. But the potential benefits greatly outweigh this risk.

[Citizen]—Kitchen Table Generals

For progressives who believe in peace through diplomacy, "kitchen table generals" are among the most difficult people to engage. We can always tell when we are with such a person by the way they quickly turn any conversation about international relations into a simple question of "nuke or not to nuke."

What is the best way for progressives to disarm these "generals?" If we just speak of "ending" a given military operation—Iraq or otherwise—that not only opens up a barrage of insults about "weakness" and Democrats wanting to "cut and run," but it actually misrepresents the progressive viewpoint on military operations.

The progressive approach to national defense in the face of current threats to our national security is based on two interconnected strategies of balance: (1) smart and strong, and (2) bringing even the weakest to the table. Both principles fall under Eisenhower's principle of "balance" in foreign policy.

To advance these strategies in a kitchen table conversation, progressives might say something like:

- For American foreign policy to be really effective—for it to really protect the country—it must seek national security in balanced strategies and policies.
- We cannot protect the American people simply by throwing everything we have in to one fight. We must be smart and strong at the same time.
- "Smart" must be balanced with "strong." The powerful must be balanced at the negotiating table by the less powerful.
- National security—like any other area of American policy—must seek progress in balance.

Eisenhower's "balance" frame may at first seem formal for the kitchen table, but it is a powerful way to set the terms for a productive discussion on national security. Once the frame has been set, the kitchen table general is free to advance as many military policies as he or she wants, but the follow up questions remain the same: "OK, but is that smart as well as strong? If we follow that initiative, will that leave us exposed on a different front? Shouldn't we, perhaps, pull back our forces, regroup, and pursue multiple fronts with a smarter, more nimble set of tactics?" The "balance" frame thus opens up a whole range of possibilities by loosening the iron grip of the kitchen table general, and redirecting the discussion to a range of progressive possibilities.

10. ASK AND ANSWER

JOHN F. KENNEDY, INAUGURAL ADDRESS (1961)[1]

Keywords: call, contrasts, country, personification, service

Strategy: Resetting the Clock—Activism as Asking—Explore the Stars

---

Quote

"In your hands, my fellow citizens, more than mine, will rest the final success or failure of our course. Since this country was founded, each generation of Americans has been summoned to give testimony to its national loyalty. The graves of young Americans who answered the call to service surround the globe. Now the trumpet summons us again-not as a call to bear arms, though arms we need—not as a call to battle, though embattled we are—but a call to bear the burden of a long twilight struggle, year in and year out, "rejoicing in hope, patient in tribulation"—a struggle against the common enemies of man: tyranny, poverty, disease and war itself. Can we forge against these enemies a grand and global alliance, North and South, East and West, that can assure a more fruitful life for all mankind? Will you join in that historic effort? In the long history of the world, only a few generations have been granted the role of defending freedom in its hour of maximum danger. I do not shrink from this

---

responsibility—I welcome it. I do not believe that any of us would exchange places with any other people or any other generation. The energy, the faith, the devotion which we bring to this endeavor will light our country and all who serve it—and the glow from that fire can truly light the world. And so, my fellow Americans: ask not what your country can do for you—ask what you can do for your country. My fellow citizens of the world: ask not what America will do for you, but what together we can do for the freedom of man."

ANALYSIS

Few speeches have achieved more iconic status than John Kennedy's 1961 Inaugural Address. Beyond delivering one of the most famous lines in any presidential speech ("Ask not what your country can do for you—ask what you can do for your country"), Kennedy framed a progressive vision of America that still resonates nearly a half-century later.

But what was the logic of Kennedy's speech that connects so strongly with the progressive worldview? To answer that question, we need to consider the "what" and "how" of Kennedy's speech: what he talked about and how he said it.

The subject of the speech is service. Nowadays, most people understand "service" to reference work in government or the military. "I thank you for your service," is a line that presidents and other politicians often use to acknowledge a government employee or military figure.

Kennedy, however, invoked the concept of service in a radically different way than as a mere acknowledgement of work done for government. He defined it instead through a visceral, dramatic metaphor delivered through haunting and memorable repetition:

[service] is [answering a call]

While Kennedy did make reference to the most traditional definition of service as enlistment in the military, he used it as a launching point for a new, more visionary idea of service as the act of asking a question and answering a call:

> Now the trumpet summons us again—not as a call to bear arms, though arms we need—not as a call to battle, though embattled we are—but a call to bear the burden of a long twilight struggle, year in and year out, 'rejoicing in hope, patient in tribulation'—a struggle against the common enemies of man: tyranny, poverty, disease and war itself.[2]

Looking closely at this passage, it becomes clear how Kennedy builds his frame through a dual use of repetition and the core metaphor of the "call." For Kennedy, repetition was a technique for emphasizing key contrasts and principles. His speech is literally filled with repetitions of a very particular kind. Rather than just saying the same word or phrase over and over again, as is the habit of President Bush, Kennedy repeats the same word or phrase as part of a pair of inverted phrases. In this passage, for example, we see the following paired repetitions:

call to bear arms < > call to bear the burden

long twilight struggle < > struggle against common enemies of man

year in < > year out

call to battle < > embattled we are

Kennedy's speech is filled with repetitions of the same phrase and inverted phrases. Looking back through the text, we can circle other repeated phrases he used that morning:

all forms of poverty < > all forms of human life

always been committed < > to which we are committed today

pay any price < > bear any burden

meet any hardship < > support any friend < > oppose any foe

we shall not always expect < > we shall always hope to find

help them < > help themselves

The list goes on and on as Kennedy used the framing technique of repetition in just about every sentence of his speech. In so doing, he drew his audience into the principle point he was making—the notion that Americans must "begin anew," and cast off traditional notions of service to embrace a new idea.

That new idea was not entirely Kennedy's invention. The personification of the idea of service had taken shape in American discourse as far back as World War I, when military recruitment envisioned the call to enlist in the form of "Uncle Sam"—the flag-turned-old-man who points at the country and says "I Want YOU." Along these lines, when Kennedy said, "Ask what you can do for your country," he created in the minds of his audience a new image, that of an individual standing up and posing a question to the country. It is difficult to see this at first—largely because Kennedy's eponymous phrase is so familiar to us—but in this phrase he is defining "service" as a conversation between two "people": an abstract idea of a citizen, and the personified notion of the "country." The country, in other words, becomes a person in Kennedy's speech. That very personal feeling that Kennedy's speech elicits, in other words, is not just the product of his Boston accent or our knowledge of his ultimate fate at the hands of a gunman. Kennedy wanted to move his audience precisely by framing the abstract notion of service in heightened personal terms.

Notice also, however, that while Americans are most familiar with the "what you can do for your country" phrase, Kennedy actually drove home his personification of service through repetition of three different versions of the word "ask"—his favorite repetition technique used in this case as a crescendo to the entire speech:

ask not what your country can do for you < > ask what you can do for your country

ask not what America will do for you < > [ask] what together we can do for the freedom of man

ask of us here the same high standards of strength and sacrifice < > [the high standards that] we ask of you

Service, in other words, is three interconnected acts of calling out to country. First, we ask what we as Americans can do for other Americans. Second, we ask what we as free citizens of the world can do for the freedom of people in general. Third, we ask that our elected leaders join us in the same high principle of service. "Ask not . . . ask . . . ask not . . . ask"—to the audience that day, the final lines of Kennedy's speech must have felt like the racing heartbeat of the "new generation," of Americans dedicated to the idea of service that Kennedy worked so hard to inspire, and that he still inspires today.

STRATEGY

[Politician]—Resetting the Clock

The nearly uninterrupted control of all three branches of the federal government from 2000-2006 by the ultra-divisive Republican Party had the effect of stripping our domestic and foreign policy of all forms of good faith negotiation and replacing it with a politics of mistrust based on confrontation and intimidation. As such, one of the monumental tasks facing the current Democratic leadership in Congress is the challenge of inspiring the nation not just to support a new set of policies, but to embrace a new style of governing.

In the week following the 2006 elections, President Bush held a round of quick meetings with Democratic leaders as an initial gesture towards what was soon to become a Democratic Party majority in the Congress. After one such meeting, and with an eye towards setting a new tone, Senator Richard Durbin (D-IL) said the following:

> We talked about our agenda, moving forward on an agenda, finding things that we can agree on to start off on the right foot. I think that's important. This is a day for looking forward, as we should, instead of looking backwards to past battles and past elections.[3]

Notice how Durbin attempted to signal to the country that Democrats would bring a new style and tone to governing by talking about politics as if it were a path on which people "start" walking forward together. Even when given just a few seconds to speak, Durbin seized upon the opportunity to frame the debate in terms of a fresh "start."

With this in mind, there is no greater example of how to set a new tone than Kennedy's inaugural address and its haunting call to "begin anew":

> So let us begin anew—remembering on both sides that civility is not a sign of weakness, and sincerity is always subject to proof. Let us never negotiate out of fear. But let us never fear to negotiate.[4]

Kennedy, of course, was calling for a new era of negotiation with the Soviet Union at the height of the Cold War—his attempt to equate American strength with a willingness to talk. Notice how Kennedy's call to "civility" begins by resetting the clock to zero, by beginning "anew." Therein lies a powerful frame for progressive candidates seeking to advance a progressive vision of strong government, at home and abroad, built on cooperation, honest dialogue, and civility. But how can this vision be expressed?

Kennedy's speech offers a great model, but the key is not to conflate his rhetorical flair with his progressive frame. Inverted repetitions can sound false and forced, but the "begin anew" frame can and should be picked back up by progressives in a broad effort to "reset the clock"—to set a new tone, a new style, a new vision for government rooted in the principle of strength through sincere dialogue.

While Kennedy's calls to "begin anew" an era of trust and cooperation referred specifically to dialogue with the Soviet Union, progressives can learn from his framing to articulate a new vision of domestic government and foreign policy for the challenges of today's divided government. For example, in a general stump speech, a progressive candidate might preface his or her specific proposals by "resetting the clock" and "stepping forward" with a new vision for government:

> For too long, our government has been weighed down by leaders who saw strength—both at home and abroad—in the false promise of intimidation, division, and confrontation. But while those leaders saw strength, the public saw only weakness. For there is no weakness more harmful to the American people, to our leaders and to our government, than the fear of talking, the fear of negotiating, the fear of sitting down at the table.

> Let's begin again and reset the clock. Let's step forward with a new American leadership that sees strength in dialogue, strength in sincerity, and strength in civility.

> Let's step forward to elect a new American leadership that tackles problems that bring us together, not problems that divide us against each other.

By framing this vision of a new government in terms of a clock starting from the top, progressives can define past divisiveness as weakness, while at the same time looking forward to the future.

[Activist]—Activism as Asking

For activists seeking to build a base for a local candidate, making it personal can be the crucial difference between success and failure. Persuading voters to support a campaign—to turn out as volunteers, to donate money, to be there on election day—is not just a challenge of getting across a platform of ideas, but of making a personal connection between an activist and a constituent. But how can this be done?

President Kennedy's inaugural address exemplifies a key framing strategy that all activists can apply: personification. Now, keep in mind that an activist should never show up on someone's doorstep and say, "Good morning, Mrs. Robinson. Ask not what your country can do for you, but what you can do for your country." That would probably solicit little more than a laugh, followed by a door slam.

However, too often progressive activists stop short of talking about activism in terms of Kennedy's metaphor of [service] is [asking and answering]. As a result, progressive calls for greater involvement from volunteers often become too impersonal to be effective. Activism, as Kennedy framed it, is first and foremost a form of service and should be talked about that way.

Consider, for example, this script from Eliot Spitzer's successful 2006 campaign for governor in New York (emphasis mine):

> If we are ever going to reform Albany, it's going to start in Lackawanna, and Saratoga Springs, and Buffalo. Because if one man can **stand up** to the powerful, so can you. **He will ask** and **you will answer**, and with one collective roar we will wake this state government right out of its long sleep and on that day government will stop being that thing we complain about and start being that thing we can do something about.[5]

Few campaign activists would consider a gubernatorial candidate's TV ads as the place to frame their appeals for more volunteers, but

Spitzer's campaign proved them wrong. In this ad, the familiar progressive logic of activism as volunteers who "help" was reframed in terms of Kennedy's metaphor of service as standing up, asking, and answering. "Ask not what Albany can do for you, but what you can do for Albany." The logic was the same, even if the words had been revised to fit the new context.

When the candidate sets the frame for campaign activism in terms of standing up, asking, and answering, door-to-door or phone-bank volunteers can then reinforce this frame by inviting people to "join the conversation" and "stand with" the candidate.

[Citizen]—Explore the Stars

One of the great moments in President Kennedy's speech comes through a call for unity of purpose and imagination in tackling the great technological, social, and intellectual challenges of his time:

> Together, let us explore the stars, conquer the deserts, eradicate disease, tap the ocean depths and encourage the arts and commerce.[6]

More than any American president, Kennedy was able to frame his speeches with the logic of people standing together and looking forward towards seemingly impossible tasks. In his time, Kennedy's optimism inspired Americans to look up and consider tackling the stars.[7] Today, it inspires us to new challenges. For example, the progressive Apollo Alliance, a non-profit group dedicated to achieving energy independence for America in ten years, takes its cue from Kennedy's infectious optimism. In their mission statement and their communications, the Apollo Alliance frames energy independence as a challenge on par with reaching the moon, and a continuation of Kennedy's call to reach for great challenges.

Beyond space travel and energy independence, how can ordinary citizens apply Kennedy's frame? One way that progressives can bring Kennedy's optimism into dinner table conversations is to initiate a discussion about tackling great problems, such as poverty, hunger, pollution, and sickness. There was a time when progressives felt inspired to speak in these larger visionary terms, but as a result of a decade of Republican talk about "trickle down economics" and "free markets," progressive creativity has been stunted. But that need not be the case.

For example, the next time a progressive joins a dinner table conversation about gas prices, he or she might seize the opportunity to frame the debate using Kennedy's logic of "exploring the stars," figuratively speaking:

> Sure gas prices are killing us right now. But I want more than low prices at the pump. I want to live in an America that stands up to the challenge of energy independence, an America that reinvents the car so that it's clean, safe and revitalizes the economy. I want an America that works fast and smart to make high gas prices a thing of the past, not because we buy more foreign oil, but because we want to move forward and face the challenge of moving beyond the technology of the past into the industries of the future.

The poetry of Kennedy's speech can turn anyone into a dinner table orator. But the key is to see that the frame of "exploring the stars" is more than just a set of well-phrased ideas. In this case, the frame opens onto a new discussion about the relationship between energy and American character. While the conversation begins with the mundane question of "gas prices," it quickly moves to a discussion of American ingenuity, resolve, and unity. And, as President Kennedy showed in launching the Apollo Project one year after his inaugural speech, which resulted in the United States landing on the moon, progressives should talk both about the challenges we face, and about the will of Americans to face these challenges precisely because they seem so difficult and vast.

11. BUILD A SOCIETY

LYNDON JOHNSON, UNIVERSITY OF MICHIGAN COMMENCEMENT ADDRESS (1964)[1]

Keywords: cities, classrooms, decay, environment, opportunity, poverty

Strategy: Building, Not Blueprint—Progressive Values—Soulless Wealth

Quote

"Your imagination, your initiative, and your indignation will deter-mine whether we build a society where progress is the servant of our needs, or a society where old values and new visions are buried un-der unbridled growth. For in your time we have the opportunity to move not only toward the rich society and the powerful society, but upward to the Great Society. The Great Society rests on abundance and liberty for all. It demands an end to poverty and racial injustice, to which we are totally committed in our time. But that is just the beginning. The Great Society is a place where every child can find knowledge to enrich his mind and to enlarge his talents. It is a place where leisure is a welcome chance to build and reflect, not a feared cause of boredom and restlessness. It is a place where the city of man serves not only the needs of the body and the demands of commerce but the desire for beauty and the hunger for community. It is a place where man can renew contact with nature. It is a place which honors creation for its own sake and for what it adds to the understanding of the race. It is a place where men are more concerned with the quality of their goals than the quantity of their goods. But most of all, the Great Society is not a safe harbor, a resting place, a final objective, a finished work. It is a challenge constantly renewed, beckoning us toward a destiny where the meaning of our lives matches the marvelous products of our labor. So I want to talk to you today about three places where we begin to build the Great Society—in our cities, in our countryside, and in our classrooms."

ANALYSIS

One of the most embattled presidents of our time, Lyndon Johnson was sworn into office following the assassination of John F. Kennedy, shepherded the country through the signing of the Civil Rights Act, and was finally elected only to have his term bloodied by the Vietnam quagmire. Despite the turmoil of his time in office, President Johnson delivered one of the last great visions for America by any president, Democrat or Republican.

Johnson's "Great Society" speech, the keynote address at the 1964 University of Michigan commencement ceremony, is a masterpiece of progressive framing for one simple reason: it articulates vision and values rather than policy. That day in May, the graduates heard President Johnson speak about the importance of "building" and rebuilding "places" in America:

> I want to talk to you today about three places where we begin to build the Great Society—in our cities, in our countryside, and in our classrooms.[2]

On first read, it may seem that this all makes good sense, as cities are in fact "places" that are "built." But what does it mean to "build" the countryside or to "build" our classrooms? This talk of "building" and "places" was in fact the core of Johnson's "Great Society" frame. The key to the frame was a series of linked metaphors that transformed potentially boring talk about government programs, legislation, and bureaucracy into a poetic and moral image:

[government program] is [a building]
[social policy] is [a building]
[cultural policy] is [a building]
[moral value] is [a building]

Just like the New Deal was a frame for a set of policies and laws designed to pull the country out of recession, the "Great Society" was Johnson's rubric for a set of policies and laws designed to eradicate urban blight, save the environment, and improve the quality of education.[3] Rather than talk about the details of actual policy, however, Johnson presented his entire vision for the country through a metaphor of "building." Grand social change in education, environment, and urban planning was in fact the product of great investment and innovation in government programs; cast in terms of the "building" metaphor, however, Johnson described these aspects of government in terms of constructing real "places."

Accordingly, the big framing lesson in Johnson's speech was the use of core metaphors to create coherence across a series of ideas. While Johnson addressed a wide range of social problems, he talked about them through the coherent logic of the "building" metaphor. The key for Johnson was identifying those "three places" where he proposed to "build" the Great Society. This set the stage for discussing such abstract notions as "values" and "community" through the coherent metaphor of a "building." Thus, the "decay" of urban centers became in Johnson's speech an image of declining values. Similarly, the pollution and deforestation of America's countryside became the equivalent of the withered "spirit" of each citizen. And the lack of growth (e.g., construction) in our education system became in Johnson's speech a way of describing the flagging quality of American public education. In each of these "three places," the moral challenges to be overcome by the "Great Society" were framed through the language of constructing "places."

Listening to Johnson's words that day, everyone in the audience would have readily understood that to "join in the battle to build the Great Society" meant to be an engaged citizen dedicated to the core progressive principles of protection and participation. Citizens were not just voters—they were builders! And the project Johnson invited them to build was no less than the all-encompassing reconstruction of the three Cs of American society: city, countryside, and classroom. All the abstract ideas of civic participation were, thus, defined by Johnson's frame in terms of concrete things:

[citizen] is [a builder]
[society] is [a building]
[social program] is [construction]
[moral value] is [good construction]
[absence of moral value] is [decay]
[material progress] is [building foundation]
[life of mind and spirit] is [building interior]

The longstanding progressive value of Johnson's "Great Society" frame, in other words, is not found solely in the specifics of the legislation that grew out of it. Johnson's real legacy was defining progressivism in terms of the hard work of building places in society that in turn strengthen the character of the nation. By building and subsequently living in the spaces of the "Great Society," America avoided becoming a society, in Johnson's words, that was "condemned to soulless wealth," and instead strived towards a civilization where every person lived a life that was rich with character and purpose. It was such a powerful vision that many progressives to this day still see themselves as "builders" of the "Great Society."

STRATEGY

[Politician]—Building, Not Blueprint

In today's confrontational politics, progressives are constantly pressed for their "plan," i.e., "What is the "Democratic plan?" This kind of question, however, is a tactical trap for candidates and elected officials, not necessarily an opportunity to show leadership.

Like blueprints for a construction job, "plans" for government projects are not the riveting stuff of public presentations or discussion. Like blueprints, plans are for engineers. What interests the public is the model of the finished project—the three-dimensional representation of the building itself.

The key lesson from Johnson's speech for candidates and elected officials is contained in this difference between blueprints and the model of the building. The public does not want to spend time looking at blueprints. They want—and deserve—a tour of the whole building. Metaphorically speaking, for a progressive candidate to switch from "blueprint" talk to "building" talk is to switch from talk about programs and individual issues to a frame of values and vision.

In light of Johnson's "Great Society" speech, progressive candidates who want to steer the debate to questions of values and visions might start by asking and answering three basic questions:

- What am I building?
- Where am I building?
- Why am I building?

The answers to these questions can help to transform "blueprint" talk into talk about the larger project. For example, a progressive candidate might have a set of policy initiatives on education that consists of greater investment in teacher training, block grants for technology in the classroom, hiring more teachers to reduce class sizes, specialized tutors to help with test skills, and meals for students from low income households. But to talk directly about those policies in a campaign speech would be to talk at the level of the "blueprint." To follow Johnson's approach, one must simply answer the three questions:

What am I building? > The world's best schools
Where am I building? > In classrooms
Why am I building? > A bright future for every child

The result is a very different approach to the progressive candidate's initial script on education:

- Our challenge is not just to improve education, but to build the world's best schools.
- When we build the best schools, every child has a place to sit, to learn, and to grow.
- In rising to this challenge, we not only build great schools, but we lay the foundation for the next generation of American leadership.

In this particular frame on education, Johnson's metaphoric coherence is extended across all three statements, articulating not just a set of policies, but a vision for education. A progressive vision for education frames a debate about excellence, equality, and leadership—not tests, computers, and salaries. Those policy details come later and in places more appropriate for unrolling blueprints.

[Activist]—Progressive Values

One of the issues that often knocks progressive activists off-balance is the aggressive way that Republicans talk about "family values." These assertions are disorienting because progressives know that while the Republican talk about values is misleading, their assertions nonetheless frame the debate and leave us on the defensive.[4]

Johnson's "Great Society" speech suggests a way out of this predicament. Midway through the speech, Johnson offered the following observation about urban expansion and decay (emphasis mine):

> Worst of all, expansion is eroding the precious and time-honored **values** of community with neighbors and communion with nature. The loss of these **values** breeds loneliness and boredom and indifference.[5]

Here, progressive activists see a very different concept of values than the one that has been repeated by Republicans for the past few decades. In Johnson's progressive worldview, "values" are "of community with neighbors" and "of communion with nature." They are the belief in the moral purpose of activities that enrich individual and group character. By contrast, Republican conceptions of "family values" are more akin to rules or requirements, i.e., marriage is only between a man and a woman.

Celebrating those activities that enrich individual and group character can be a powerful tool for activists. For example, a group of volunteers for a progressive candidate might be asked to make phone calls on the subject of education and the environment to prospective voters. Rather than talking about the candidates' policy proposals, the activists might instead initiate a conversation about the values that progressives believe in:

- We believe that great education strengthens the values of respect for neighbors and service to community.
- We believe in the values of people working to preserve and to enjoy the American outdoors.
- We believe in the values of teaching new technology rooted in the ideas of our American heritage.
- We believe in the values of fostering individual creativity and responsibility.

The particular values that a campaign wishes to articulate can be decided through group brainstorming sessions, and will vary from campaign to campaign and from candidate to candidate. The key, however, is realizing that progressive values are framed not as rules for conduct, but as beliefs in the moral purpose of activities that enrich the lives of American citizens. Or as Johnson might define them, progressive values are the "foundations" of the "Great Society."

[Citizen]—Soulless Wealth

A conviction that all progressives share is the belief that excessive material wealth for its own sake is anathema to a healthy society. For this reason, every progressive relishes the dinner table conversation about the "excesses" of wealth. But what is this topic ultimately about? How should it be framed? Johnson answered these very questions at the outset of his speech:

> the Great Society is not a safe harbor, a resting place, a final objective, a finished work. It is a challenge constantly renewed, beckoning us toward a destiny where the meaning of our lives matches the marvelous products of our labor.[6]

For Johnson the opposite of the Great Society was an America of "soulless wealth"—riches without purpose, material means without meaning. And therein lay the seed of a powerful frame for discussion of progressive views on wealth and responsibility.

An ideal subject for invoking this frame of "soulless wealth" is the stock market. In a dinner table conversation that turns to the markets rising to historic levels, for example, a progressive might leap in and say:

> It's great when American companies are doing well, as that provides more jobs and more possibilities for everyone. But I wonder if these huge gains from the market—these windfall profits—I wonder if this wealth isn't soulless? I believe we can use this wealth to invest in solving the problems that

are in front of us, the problems of health, environment, energy, and religious conflict. I believe that we have the power to shape the society we want, not just to make money.

Framing a conversation about stock market profit in terms of "soulless wealth" is a strategy for driving the conversation towards progressive ideas. But it can also reflect a much broader strategy for channeling actual wealth towards progressive goals. In the past few years, for example, the Clinton Global Initiative has framed the idea of wealth in terms remarkably similar to Johnson's Great Society, albeit at the level of a global society.[7]

On both the micro and the macro level, the difference between progressive and conservative ideas about wealth, can be characterized as a difference between principles and principal. Conservatives value the amassing of financial capital above all other economic motivations, whether in regard to personal behavior or government action. Progressives, by contrast, are concerned with principled spending and investing, the purpose of wealth being the general progress of the individual as a member of society. These two distinctions have radical consequences for discussions of markets, growth, and capital. Quite often, however, conservatives will make the mistake of believing that progressives are opposed to the accumulation of wealth when, in fact, what progressives oppose is soulless wealth—capitalism based on principal, but not principles.

12. I HAVE SUCCEEDED

RICHARD NIXON, RESIGNATION SPEECH (1974)[1]

Keywords: association, boasting, misdirection, spin, work

Strategy: Swiftboating—Trolls—Trains Run on Time

Quote

"For more than a quarter of a century in public life, I have shared in the turbulent history of this evening. I have fought for what I believe in. I have tried, to the best of my ability, to discharge those duties and meet those responsibilities that were entrusted to me. Sometimes I have succeeded. And sometimes I have failed. But always I have taken heart from what Theodore Roosevelt once said about the man in the arena, whose face is marred by dust and sweat and blood, who strives valiantly, who errs and comes short again and again because there is not effort without error and shortcoming, but who does actually strive to do the deed, who knows the great enthusiasms, the great devotions, who spends himself in a worthy cause, who at the best knows in the end the triumphs of high achievements and with the worst if he fails, at least fails while daring greatly. I pledge to you tonight that as long as I have a breath of life in my body, I shall continue in that spirit. I shall continue to work for the great causes to which I have been dedicated throughout my years as a Congressman, a Senator, Vice President and President, the cause of peace—not just for America but among all nations—prosperity, justice and opportunity for all of our people. There is one cause above all to which I have been devoted and to which I shall always be devoted for as long as I live. When I first took the oath of office as President five and a half years ago, I made this sacred commitment: to consecrate my office, my energies, and all the wisdom I can summon to the cause of peace among nations. I've done my very best in all the days since to be true to that pledge. As a result of these efforts, I am confident that the world is a safer place today, not only for the people of America but for the people of all nations, and that all of our children have a better chance than before of living in peace rather than dying in war."

ANALYSIS

At first, it may seem unlikely that there could be framing lessons relevant to progressives in a speech by Richard Nixon—let alone in his resignation speech. Yet, Nixon's resignation speech demonstrates one of the most important lessons for progressives: the difference between framing and "spin." [2]

Good framing in a speech prunes away the distractions so that the vision grows fuller and more vibrant, giving the listener a better chance to appreciate the ideas being expressed. Spin, by contrast, distracts the listener through misdirection.

In his farewell speech, Nixon uses three key rhetorical devices that constitute spin:

- Misdirection
- Boasting
- Association

Taken together, these three techniques are successful because they send up an emotionally compelling smokescreen.

The act of misdirection came by invoking the "work" frame. To most Americans, the resignation speech was about the criminality of the president—a shocking revelation without rival in the 20th Century. But to Nixon, the subject of the speech was not crime, but work. The following phrases in the speech invoked the "work" frame:

- "I have never been a quitter."
- "America needs a full-time President and a full-time Congress"
- "I will not be here in this office working on your behalf."

The "work" frame was invoked so strongly that a person turning in who knew nothing of the Watergate scandal might have thought they were watching a speech about the virtues of employment. Drawing people's attention to the idea of "work"—the need for work, the importance of work, the nature of work—was Nixon's attempt at misdirection. "Don't look at the crimes I've committed," he was saying, "just look at the work I've done."

Misdirection can be devastating to an audience's ability to stay focused on the subject at hand, and it can be quite effective in influencing opinion. For example, while most progressives believe that the nation is uniform in its conviction that Richard Nixon resigned in disgrace, many Americans still view him as a hard working President with a long list of accomplishments that were cut short by the Watergate scandal. Indeed, one of the goals of misdirection is to control the long-term interpretation of events—to cloud future readings of immoral acts by framing them in terms that distract from the truth.

The key to the long-term success of Nixon's misdirection was the second spin device he used in his speech: boasting. Boasting? What did a president who resigned in shame have to boast about? Yet, if we listen to Nixon's speech carefully, we see that it is among the most boastful presidential speeches ever written. And that is because "boasting" of accomplishments is a key element of the strategy to spin failure into success.

In the speech, Nixon boasted of no less than four major foreign policy achievements:

- Ending the Vietnam War ("We have ended America's longest war.")
- Diplomacy with China ("We have unlocked the doors")
- Diplomacy with the Middle East ("100 million people . . . now look at us as friends.")
- Nuclear Treaty with the Soviet Union ("The threat of nuclear war will no longer hang over the world.")

Nixon's logic was to pile a set of accomplishments so high that it would outshine the small fact that he had broken the law and faced impeachment. In one hand: a crime. In the other hand: global diplomacy, an end to the conflict in Vietnam, an end to the threat of nuclear war with the Soviet Union. Balanced against one another, the crime doesn't seem so bad—or at least that was what the spin wanted to show.

Moreover, Nixon framed his accomplishments as if "we"—the American people—had achieved them along with him. "We have ended," "we have unlocked," "we must continue"—over a dozen times, Nixon described his own accomplishments as if they had been a group effort. The irony, of course, was that the Nixon presidency was among the most secretive and divisive of all administrations—few Americans ever felt they were working with him to accomplish anything. Yet, in listening to him that night, we could have easily begun to feel that this was a speech about our accomplishments—tragically cut short by Watergate.

However effective and extensive his misdirection, Nixon's spin was not complete until he invoked the device of "association," by aligning himself with other great figures in American history. By invoking the name of another famous Republican president, Theodore Roosevelt,

Nixon made the case that the crimes he had committed were not in fact faults, but rather the marks of a great man, the kind of figure Roosevelt had referred to as the "man in the arena":

> Always I have taken heart from what Theodore Roosevelt once said about the man in the arena, whose face is marred by dust and sweat and blood, who strives valiantly, who errs and comes short again and again because there is not effort without error and shortcoming, but who does actually strive to do the deed, who knows the great enthusiasms, the great devotions, who spends himself in a worthy cause, who at the best knows in the end the triumphs of high achievements and with the worst if he fails, at least fails while daring greatly.[3]

Nixon's reference to Roosevelt's speech was an astounding moment of presidential chutzpah. The point of Roosevelt's speech about the "man in the arena"—which Roosevelt delivered shortly after his presidency had ended—was to say that it is the person who works hard to achieve great things, the great man, who counts, not the critics who find fault with him.[4] By framing himself with Roosevelt's words, Nixon claimed for himself the status of a great man—in the very speech in which he resigned on account of the crimes he had committed.

One cannot help but sit back and marvel at Nixon's spin, and at the ease by which he transformed a speech about his own crimes against the constitution and the American people into a celebration of his tireless and unceasing greatness and hard work. And, to this day, the spin that Nixon floated in that speech still hangs in the American psyche. Even the most vocal of Nixon's critics often concede that while he may have violated the constitution, he was a great diplomat and a strong leader. The resignation spin is not by itself responsible for keeping Nixon's reputation inside this frame, but it was a key factor.

Nixon's resignation speech stands as a classic example of spin designed to deflect blame from the speaker in order to elevate or increase his or her standing. In contemporary politics, by contrast, the vast majority of spin is designed to lower or diminish the status of another candidate or group in the mind of the listener—in other words: the voter. When aimed at others, the goal of spin is to misdirect, smear, and associate. While the desired outcome is the opposite of what Nixon intended, the tactic is the same.

STRATEGY

[Politician]—Swiftboating

In recent years, "swiftboating" has become one of the most dangerous forms of spin used by Republicans against progressives. The term comes from the name of the non-profit group Swift Boat Veterans for Truth that ran a series of ads in the 2004 presidential election claiming that John Kerry had lied about his heroism as a swift boat captain in Vietnam. Once "swiftboated," the virtues of a candidate— their military heroism, their generosity or truthfulness—become irrevocably stained by the spin of the opposition.[5]

Lately, however, Republican swiftboat attacks have begun to fall short. In the 2006 election race for Pennsylvania's Eighth congressional district, for example, an attempt by the incumbent Republican Mike Fitzpatrick to question the military service of the Democratic challenger Patrick Murphy backfired when Murphy fought back.[6] In the end, Murphy won the election. But despite some recent failed attempts, Republican swiftboat attacks remain dangerous political tactics that can destroy a campaign.

To fight this kind of spin, progressives must take the initiative to ensure they stay in their own frame. And to do that, they can examine Nixon's spin tactics to understand how "swiftboating" works and to how disarm it.

Like Nixon's speech, all swiftboating begins with misdirection. The goal of a swiftboat attack is to misdirect voters away from the actual issues at hand and redirect them to the falsified personal shortcomings of the targeted candidate. For example, in a debate about the failed Iraqi occupation and a Republican candidate's blind support of President Bush, suddenly a television ad airs saying that the progressive candidate assaulted a woman in Vietnam. To disarm misdirection, progressives should not respond to the accusation, but instead shine a light on the spin:

- My opponent does not want to talk about the failed Iraq war that he supported, so he has **shined a spotlight on me instead**.
- My opponent wants us to **turn away** from the real debate and talk about false charges.
- Through a **sleight of hand**, my opponent has us talking about the spin he made up about me, when just yesterday we were debating Iraq.

The next step is to battle the smear by invoking the frame of swift-boaters as immoral "gangs" who use threats to intimidate and silence opposition. Gangs succeed by disrupting the moral accounting of American life. This is a popular theme in American mythology, particularly in accounts of the nineteenth century western frontier. A progressive candidate should emphasize that when we work hard and play by the rules, we deserve to have our voices heard, not silenced by "political gangs":

- This campaign will not be **threatened by political gangs** trying to silence the people.
- I will not be silenced by my opponents' **political gangs**.
- Together, the people of [state, county, city, etc.] and I will **not be bullied by my opponents' political gangs.** We will continue the fight for real issues, and real change.

To defang a swiftboat attack, in other words, a progressive candidate should frame the attack in terms of the morality of the people fighting the immorality of the lawless. This "people vs. gangs" frame is not only easy to invoke, but quickly understood, because it is a common theme in American history.

And, just as Nixon associated himself with great leaders before him, swiftboaters drive home their spin by "associating" progressive candidates with nefarious and dangerous people or groups. To avoid this trap, a progressive candidate must take control of the story by talking to the media in order to get the focus back on the differences in the campaign. In an interview on a talk show, for example, a candidate under swiftboat attack might say the following:

- Nobody enjoys all this negative attention.
- I can see that my opponent would rather have his political gangs distract us than focus on the real issues in this race.
- I am happy to talk about my service in the military, but let's turn the spotlight back where it was before I was attacked: Iraq.
- Unlike my opponent, I served in the military. Unlike my opponent, I believe in an immediate change in our Iraq policy. Unlike my opponent, I believe the President must be held to account for mistakes made in this war and in this occupation.

Accordingly, swiftboating loses its power when a strong light is shined on it and an even swifter effort is made to reclaim the momentum in the debate. The result is that the spin of the swiftboat campaign is defused, and the debate is once again directed towards articulating progressive values.

[Activist]—Trolls

A particular form of spin that online activists face almost every day are attacks from conservative "trolls."[7] Trolls are agitators who visit progressive online communities and then use inflammatory comments to disrupt and derail discussion. In addition to being simply annoying, trolls work with a very specific goal in mind: to undermine the productive exchange of ideas by luring and trapping progressives inside conservative spin. Being "hit" by a troll in a discussion almost always results in an angry "flame war"—the online version of a bare-knuckle fistfight.

Nixon's resignation speech, while not the work of a troll, can help progressives see that trolls succeed by using the same tactic of misdirection. Whereas Nixon's misdirection changed the focus from the crimes he committed to the "work" "we" accomplished, conservative trolls nowadays typically use two kinds of misdirection:

- Attack the liberal—"liberals are the **real** racists!"
- Hate Labeling—"Why do you **hate** the President so much?"

Both forms of misdirection enable the troll to control the discussion by turning it into a confrontation. Progressives accused of racism, for example, tend to respond by putting up a defensive: "I am not!"

One way to re-frame a troll is not to be defensive, but to "shine light" on the misdirection, then frame the troll's comments as a political tactic. Some questions that can be used to "shine light" on the misdirection are:

- "What do you mean by 'racism' (e.g., the term used to misdirect) in this case?"
- "Why are we suddenly discussing liberals who 'hate' America?"
- "When did this discussion stop being about Iraq and start being about liberals?"

The next step is to frame the interruption as a "hijacking" of the conversation, thereby placing the troll outside the discussion:

These comments are a political tactic intended to hijack this discussion.

By seeing the troll's comments as an attempt at misdirection, progressive activists can retain control of the discussion without engaging in a no-win argument designed to silence debate. The results are not always perfect, but the lessons from Nixon's resignation speech can help us anticipate and prepare for the interruption.

[Citizen]—Trains Run On Time

In conversations about politicians who have committed immoral or illegal acts while in office, progressives often find themselves presented with the same "boasting" frame that Nixon used in his resignation speech. The "boasting" frame attempts to relocate the discussion of a crime to a broad discussion of political achievement. Nixon did this in his resignation speech by boasting of his so-called achievements as a diplomat. Another classic example of the "boasting" frame is how supporters of Benito Mussolini used to sidestep all discussion of his crimes with the phrase, "But he made the trains run on time." Of course, Mussolini did not actually make the trains run on time, but the point of "boasting" is not to present facts, but to hijack the debate.[8] In other words, no matter how bad Mussolini—or Nixon—was, no matter how many crimes they committed, the debate becomes trapped in a frame about their good work.

In a dinner table conversation, progressives will often find themselves listening to a supporter of a politician who committed a crime attempting to use the "boasting" frame to misdirect the debate. When faced with this type of frame, progressives should respond by invoking the "still guilty" frame—a clear and straightforward tactic for bumping the discussion back into the criminality of the politician in question. If one were faced with a conversation where a Republican was defending Nixon on the basis of his work in international relations, a progressive might reframe the debate by saying:

- "Sure he did some good work as a diplomat, but he was **still a criminal**."

- "Crimes against the Constitution and the American people are **not expunged** by good deeds."
- "A crook with a long resume is still **a crook**."

Keep in mind that diehard supporters of convicted or indicted politicians are rarely swayed even by good framing. However, a dinner table discussion often includes more people than just those doing the talking—it also includes the people who are listening. The goal, then, is not to respond with a knockout punch that will bring the send the claims crashing to the canvas, but to use the opportunity to define an alterative frame that can influence others who are observing the conversation.[9]

13. DOWN THAT PATH

JIMMY CARTER, TELEVISED ADDRESS TO THE NATION (1979)[1]

Keywords: crisis, confidence, doubt, energy, progress, vision

Strategy: Talk to the People—Faith in Progress—Smear Campaigns

Quote

"The erosion of our confidence in the future is threatening to destroy the social and the political fabric of America [...] We are at a turning point in our history. There are two paths to choose. One is a path I've warned about tonight, the path that leads to fragmentation and self- interest. Down that road lies a mistaken idea of freedom, the right to grasp for ourselves some advantage over others. That path would be one of constant conflict between narrow interests ending in chaos and immobility. It is a certain route to failure. All the traditions of our past, all the lessons of our heritage, all the promises of our future point to another path, the path of common purpose and the restoration of American values. That path leads to true freedom for our Nation and ourselves. We can take the first steps down that path as we begin to solve our energy problem. Energy will be the immediate test of our ability to unite this Nation, and it can also be the standard around which we rally. On the battlefield of energy we can win for our Nation a new confidence, and we can seize control again of our common destiny."

ANALYSIS

One of the most difficult tasks faced by any President is the "crisis" speech, where bad news has to be communicated to the American people. "A hurricane just destroyed the Gulf Coast," "The war is not going well," "The country was been attacked." The topic in a crisis speech is never good news.

One of the most famous presidential crisis speeches was delivered by President Jimmy Carter on July 15, 1979. Known as the "Crisis of Confidence" speech, the bad news Carter needed to deliver was that the country was "in a dangerous energy crisis." With gas lines, rising prices, and spiraling interest rates, Carter set out to calm the concerns of the country and to lay out a series of proposals that would attempt to balance the markets, shore up supplies, and give people a sense of direction for the future.

Carter's speech was both passionate and heartfelt, including not only the specifics of government programs he planned to initiate, but also quotes from recent conversations he had had with ordinary citizens. Reminiscent of the promise of George Washington to listen to the "voice" of his country, Carter explained that the energy crisis was in fact part of a broader moral and emotional crisis.

Still, despite the common reading that Carter's speech was powerful because it tied energy to the very personal idea of "confidence," the real power in his speech came through the logic he invoked to define "crisis"—the "Path" frame.

If we listen closely to what President Carter was saying about the crisis in the country, we notice that he began his speech by saying that the country was in a very deep hole:

> It's clear that the true problems of our Nation are much deeper—deeper than gasoline lines or energy shortages, deeper even than inflation or recession. And I realize more than ever that as President I need your help. So, I decided to reach out and listen to the voices of America.

In reading a presidential speech to understand the logic of the frame, repetition of a word typically draws our attention, and this case is no exception. By repeating the word "deeper" several times in this paragraph, Carter was invoking a particular metaphor:

[crisis] is [a hole]

The metaphor may seem mundane when diagrammed, but it was the key to Carter's framing strategy for the speech.[2] The energy problems the nation faced, he argued, were not just economic processes, but were best understood in spatial terms: that is, the nation was "deep" inside a crisis that threatened American democracy:

> The threat is nearly invisible in ordinary ways. It is a crisis of confidence. It is a crisis that strikes at the very heart and soul and spirit of our national will. We can see this crisis in the growing doubt about the meaning of our own lives and in the loss of a unity of purpose for our Nation. The erosion of our confidence in the future is threatening to destroy the social and the political fabric of America.[3]

What we see in this passage is not just the familiar "crisis of confidence" phrase, but also the logic of the [crisis] is [a hole] metaphor that Carter invoked using the phrases "growing doubt" and "erosion." After listening to the voice of the American people, he understood that the nation was in a "deep" crisis that had "eroded" the solid ground of confidence on which the country had stood for two centuries. While the surface of democracy was still there, but it was above us.

The [crisis] is [a hole] logic may seem peculiar when teased out of Carter's speech, but in fact we draw on it all the time to talk about our problems, as we speak about all kinds of crises in terms of holes: to have an emotional crisis is to be "in a deep funk;" to have a financial crisis is to be "deep in debt;" and so forth. Our entire conception of what a crisis means is expressed through the spatial dynamics of a hole. As such, Americans listening to Carter's speech would have understood immediately what he meant. And, they would have understood what needed to come next—that the logical antithesis of the [crisis] is [a hole] metaphor was:

[the solution to a crisis] is [a path out of the hole]

Once he framed the energy crisis as a deep hole in America's moral and spiritual self-confidence, Carter then reinforced this notion through a series of very powerful quotes from average Americans, which showed that the hole we were in was much bigger and much deeper than just the economics of the bottomed-out markets. Then, further reinforcing his frame, Carter talked about the solution, the "path" back up to the surface, back up to confidence:

> We are at a turning point in our history. There are two paths to choose. One is a path I've warned about tonight, the path that leads to fragmentation and self-interest. Down that road lies a mistaken idea of freedom, the right to grasp for ourselves some advantage over others. That path would be one of constant conflict between narrow interests ending in chaos and immobility. It is a certain route to failure.[4]

The logical coherence that Carter invoked through this part of his speech was nothing short of remarkable. The crisis of confidence, we see, was not just a hole, but a canyon that had opened up in the wake of the Watergate scandal and had left the country in doubt about its continued ability to overcome its problems. Trapped in that canyon, there were two possible paths to choose:

> the path deeper into the crisis, and the path out. Carter cho-sen path emphasized his "crisis" frame and implicitly invoked Robert Frost's famous poem "The Road Not Taken."[5]

The central policy initiatives of Carter's speech focused on conservation, innovation, and moderation. To get the country out of its energy crisis, Carter asked the country to wean itself off foreign oil and excessive use of fuel through a series of measures that entailed a change in the American lifestyle. When his proposals are seen through the prism of the [hole] and [path] metaphors, we can begin to understand the larger strategy of Carter's framing, which was to rally the American people by moving beyond economic questions to questions of American character and resolve. "You know we can do it," he urged. "We have the natural resources . . . we have the most skilled work force . . . we have the national will to win this war." With confidence eroded, he was saying, the American people were in a deep hole, and they had to choose a path out, and dedicate themselves to rebuilding their confidence with the strength and energy usually reserved for a war effort. In this respect, Carter also invoked a frame of [national participation] as [war], a frame that Franklin Roosevelt had invoked when he attempted to rally the American public out of the great hole of his time, the Great Depression, which was also described by Roosevelt as a crisis of American confidence and resolve.

STRATEGY

[Politician]—Talk to the People

In the past twenty years, it has become *de rigueur* for presidents to plant ordinary citizens in the audience and then refer to them during a speech, or to host a "Town Hall" meeting that places the president in front of a group of ordinary Americans. Despite these carefully staged and managed events, Americans have grown skeptical of the idea that a sitting president actually knows or interacts with regular citizens. Most of us see these references to the "everyday Joe" in a speech or a campaign stop as little more than a communications gimmick.

However, Carter's "Crisis of Confidence" speech suggests an

entirely different approach to this tactic. Rather than referring to an "average" person in the audience, Carter framed his entire speech in terms of listening to the American people. The key difference for Carter, however, was that he did not just plant a person in the audience in order to boast about the success of a government program. Rather, his speech invoked the idea of a President who values the voice of the people—a core progressive principle and the very frame of the Constitution. For Carter, speaking to the people was not a metaphor, but an event, which he referenced and quoted in his speech. The result is a two-stage approach vis-à-vis "talk to the people":

- Talk to the people (actual event)
- Talk about talking to the people (content of speech)

Collapsing this distinction between talk as an event and talk as speech content is detrimental to progressives because it reduces the American people to political stage props instead of elevating them to the status of participants in democracy—and participation is one of the most important progressive principles.

To maintain this two-stage approach to "talk to the people," progressive candidates and elected officials can consider a variety of events that precede a particular speech and which offer a real opportunity for interaction. Senator Russ Feingold (D-WI), for example, regularly hosts talking sessions with his constituents in Wisconsin to listen to their views on current issues. Former Senator John Edwards regularly meets with local organizers to hear them talk about the challenges of fighting poverty. In an age where email lists and national conference calls are often substitutes for actual "face time," progressives should follow Carter's example and actually invite people to a place—either a physical place or an interactive online place—where they can talk and be heard. Then, having heard people talk, progressive candidates and officials can include the real "voice" of the people in their speeches. Rather than gesturing to the people, while taking away their voice, progressives can engage the people by presenting their actual words and ideas. The key phrases Carter used by way of including the voices of the people are still valuable reference points for current progressives:

- "I want to share with you what I've heard."
- "Let me quote a few of the typical comments that I wrote down."
- "This from a young woman in Pennsylvania."
- "This kind of summarized a lot of other statements."
- "I have a notebook full of comments and advice. I'll read just a few."
- "And this is one of the most vivid statements."
- "And the last that I'll read."

These phrases are the rhetorical road signs Carter used in his speech to direct his audience to the voice of the people. Such phrases are decidedly more effective at advancing a progressive vision than the current habit of singling out an audience member and then speaking for them.

Ultimately, the events and phrases a progressive candidate chooses will pertain to the needs of each office and the particular ideas in focus. But recognizing in Carter's "Crisis of Confidence" speech a basic two-stage approach to "talk to the people" is a crucial framing insight.

[Activist]—Faith In Progress

"Faith" is a crucial issue that often vexes progressive activists. This frustration is not because progressives are anti-religious, but because the entire Republican "noise-machine" spends an inordinate amount of time and money accusing progressives of conducting a "war" on religion. Not surprisingly, this has left progressive activists frustrated. Yet "faith" is not only a fundamentally progressive frame for talking about America, it is also a broad and welcoming frame for understanding democracy itself. Carter's "Crisis of Confidence" speech exemplifies how this concept can be used to advance a progressive vision of America:

> Confidence has defined our course and has served as a link between generations. We've always believed in something called progress. We've always had faith that the days of our children would be better than our own. Our people are losing that faith, not only in government itself but in the ability as citizens to serve as the ultimate rulers and shapers of our democracy. As a people we know our past and we are proud of it. Our progress has been part of the living history of America, even the world. [6]

This passage should be printed out and pasted on the refrigerator of every progressive activist in America, as it is not only a fundamental statement of what progressive activists work hard to achieve every day, but also expresses a long-term aspiration of the progressive movement, which is to restore confidence to the American people. Whether they are religious or not (and progressives believe that is a choice left up to each individual), all activists share a dedication to the idea of confidence as framed by Carter: [Confidence] is faith in progress. Progressives believe that the future will be even better than the present. Progressives have faith in the idea of government, and our own abilities, to bring that bright future to fruition. Thus, when faced with assertions about their so-called hostility to people of faith, progressive activists can draw on Carter's ideas to reclaim the debate:

> "Faith? Faith in America is about much more than religion. Faith speaks to the core beliefs that all Americans once held: faith that our children's lives would be better than our own, faith in good government, faith in democracy, and faith in each other. Progressives have never lost that faith. And we work hard every day to restore it in this country."

Activists can play an important role in reframing the idea of faith in American political debate. And that reframing can help to drive public discussions towards the very ideals that progressive candidates advocate.

[Citizen]—Smear Campaigns

Every progressive dreads the "October surprise"—the last minute smear campaign that comes out of nowhere with the intention of distracting the voters and forcing the candidate into a defensive position. In many cases, these campaigns take the form of a "blast-from-the-past" factoid about a progressive candidate's personal life. Unfortunately, these kinds of smears lead to conversations dominated by the cynical "they're all the same," theme. According to this logic, all politicians—Republican or Democrat—are the "same" in that they are all corrupt and hide past indiscretions.

When faced with these usually false accusations, it is often difficult to deliver a response that drives the debate back towards progressive values and vision. Carter's "Crisis of Confidence" speech offers a good model for framing an "October surprise" in order to regain control of the debate. The key is remembering that President Carter drew on a very particular metaphor to frame a "crisis":

> [crisis] is [a hole]

The coherence of this logic was reinforced through words that described a crisis in terms of being "down in" or "deep in" a set of problems.[7]

Most scandals are also commonly understood in terms of the [crisis] as [a hole] metaphor. In the midst of a successful campaign, for example, a progressive candidate may suddenly find him or herself "down" or "deep in" trouble, unable to "get out of" the "hole" created by a smear campaign. Seeing this logic is important because it shifts our focus away from worrying about correcting past mistakes and towards finding the path out of the hole. For example, the next time a progressive finds him or herself in a dinner table conversation with someone who says, "They're all the same—Republican, Democrat . . . they're all corrupt," they can respond by invoking the "path" frame:

> Well, I don't agree that all candidates are the same. For example, unlike conservatives, progressives look forward, not back. This race is at a turning point. There are two paths to choose. One path takes us back to questions that turn us against each other, to cynicism, to frustration. The other path leads us forward, to a focus not on what was said, but on what is being done to bring about change for the better. While nobody is perfect, and we have all said things at one point that we regret, what really matters is the path we have taken since then.

There are many other ways to invoke the "path" frame, but the important point to note is how the logic of starting points and moving forward can be instrumental in pulling the debate out of the hole a smear campaign creates.

14. A SMALL STORY

RONALD REAGAN, FAREWELL ADDRESS TO THE NATION (1989)[1]

Keywords: audience, communicating, grandfather, policy, promise

Strategy: Set the Stage—Big Meaning—Small Things—
The Dinner Table

Quote

"I've been reflecting on what the past eight years have meant and mean. And the image that comes to mind like a refrain is a nautical one—a small story about a big ship, and a refugee, and a sailor. It was back in the early eighties, at the height of the boat people. And the sailor was hard at work on the carrier Midway, which was patrolling the South China Sea. The sailor, like most American servicemen, was young, smart, and fiercely observant. The crew spied on the horizon a leaky little boat. And crammed inside were refugees from Indochina hoping to get to America. The Midway sent a small launch to bring them to the ship and safety. As the refugees made their way through the choppy seas, one spied the sailor on deck, and stood up, and called out to him. He yelled, 'Hello, American sailor. Hello, freedom man.' A small moment with a big meaning, a moment the sailor, who wrote it in a letter, couldn't get out of his mind.

> And, when I saw it, neither could I. Because that's what it was to be an American in the 1980's. We stood, again, for freedom. I know we always have, but in the past few years the world again—and in a way, we ourselves—rediscovered it. It's been quite a journey this decade, and we held together through some stormy seas. And at the end, together, we are reaching our destination."

ANALYSIS

For many conservatives, Ronald Reagan was the greatest American leader to emerge in the twentieth century—an inspiring speaker (nicknamed "The Great Communicator") who restored American pride at home and abroad, championed traditional values, and ended the cold war. Most progressives, by contrast, see Reagan not only as a bad communicator, but as a divisive leader who waged a relentless campaign against America's faith in good government, decimated the middle class, and gave rise to a new form of dangerous American arrogance in global politics.

Neither side, however, has spent enough time understanding the incredible gift that Reagan had for framing a debate. In truth, one need not admire or admonish Reagan's policies in order to learn from his framing. And, in terms of framing, his Farewell Address to the Nation, delivered on January 11, 1989, was perhaps his most noteworthy speech, primarily because of the "story time" frame.

While past presidents usually summed up their years in office by speaking in the idiom of the senior statesman, Reagan presented his closing remarks through the logic of a wise old man telling meaningful stories to a group of people gathered at his feet. To initiate the "story time" frame, Reagan invited his audience to join him as he gazed longingly through the windows of his presidency out onto the story of a new and hopeful America:

> You know, down the hall and up the stairs from this office is the part of the White House where the President and his

family live. There are a few favorite windows I have up there that I like to stand and look out of early in the morning. The view is over the grounds here to the Washington Monument, and then the Mall and the Jefferson Memorial. But on mornings when the humidity is low, you can see past the Jefferson to the river, the Potomac, and the Virginia shore. Someone said that's the view Lincoln had when he saw the smoke rising from the Battle of Bull Run. I see more prosaic things: the grass on the banks, the morning traffic as people make their way to work, now and then a sailboat on the river. I've been thinking a bit at that window. I've been reflecting on what the past eight years have meant and mean.[2]

These images framed Reagan as much more than an aging President about to pass the torch to the next leader. Through a stage set by his own words, Reagan became a great poet king staring out over his dominion, a wise and benevolent ruler who yearned for beauty, not legacy, who saw only the land, and worried little about the intricacies of politics. By opening and closing his speech with this same image of him staring out the window, Reagan was saying to his audience: "Come with me through the looking glass, and I will tell you a story about America."

However, in the "story time" frame, the meaning of the individual stories is less important than the logic invoked—what Reagan described as seeing "a small moment with a big meaning." To him, that refugee standing up and calling out to the American sailor meant that "We stood, again, for freedom." The power of Reagan's "story time" frame was that he asked nothing more from his audience than that they suspend their critical thinking while he told them how individual "small" moments in a world of uncertainty stood for the greatness of America. The ability to frame the tiniest details as if they were the whole of American promise was Reagan's great gift as a speaker. Or, as he phrased it later in the speech, "Life has a way of reminding you of big things through small incidents."

Reagan's "story time" frame also colored his view of government and politics in the rosy glow of intimacy. To establish that intimacy, Reagan drew on a few key metaphors to communicate his definition of politics:

[political vision] is [gazing out a window]
[political diplomacy] is [making friends]
[politic debate] is [dinner table conversation]
[political ideology] is [a warm feeling]

Each one of these metaphors was invoked through a small story or small lesson that Reagan shared in the speech. In one story, he recalled a diplomatic summit during which world leaders addressed each other on a first name basis. In another, he reminded us that the first "lesson about America" is that all change begins at the dinner table. And, in several other stories, he reflected on the warm feelings of patriotism and freedom that had returned to America under his watch. Reagan's farewell speech exemplifies the power of personalizing the most complex political processes in terms of small, everyday experiences.

The "story time" frame also served another purpose, which was to draw people's attention away from the problematic policies of the Reagan administration, and the deep contradictions of the man himself. For example, while Reagan gazed out windows at beautiful landscapes, he was blind to the urban poor right in front of him. While he viewed diplomacy as friendship with foreign diplomats, he broke the law to sell arms to Iran in exchange for hostages. Reagan believed that all change took place at the dinner table, yet gutted social programs that left more and more people with no food on that table. And while Reagan believed deeply that conservative ideology created an intimate feeling in the heart of Americans, at no time in recent history did Americans feel more distant from their government, from their communities, and from themselves. Reagan's metaphors were an embodiment of his huge contradictions as a President—a man who was warm of manner, but brutal of policy.

Despite this, the very personal metaphors that Reagan used in the speech created a real engagement between the listener and the abstractions of politics. Bureaucratic pretense dissipated, as did the often-daunting jargon of current events. We were invited to see participation in politics as no more complicated than sitting down at the table for a conversation—no more difficult than sitting in the dark for a Hollywood matinee.

In the end, though most progressives disagree with Reagan's policies, it is difficult to dismiss the profound lesson that his frames hold for us. Indeed, "small things" can and often do have big meaning, and the ability to walk away from policy talk and just tell a story is a skill that, unfortunately, too few progressives cultivate.

STRATEGY

[Politician]—Set The Stage

One of the most admirable qualities of just about every progressive candidate or elected official is their insatiable desire to make politics about facts and policies. If most progressive candidates had their way, every speech would cut right to the facts of why progressive policies are the best way to restore confidence in America, improve our economy, protect our citizens, educate our children, and care for our planet. However, the problem with leading with facts and policies is that even the most ardent progressive supporter appreciates it when a candidate or elected official first "sets the stage."

President Reagan's Farewell Speech to the Nation is an excellent example of what it means to "set the stage." In the speech, every point Reagan made depended on his first placing the mind of the audience on a particular "stage" and a particular "set." For Reagan, the stage was the White House and the set was his favorite staircase and a window that looked out over the Jefferson Memorial to the Potomac River. This stage and set were critical because they contextualized the audience's understanding of the key issues of pride, hope, and freedom, and provided a visceral understanding of the "small moments" with "big meaning" that framed the speech.

Setting the stage for a speech is always important. Consider, for example, a progressive candidate giving a speech about the importance of raising the minimum wage—a policy that needs to be stated in the form of a fact, i.e. the specific dollar amount of the proposed wage increase. How might that candidate "set the stage" for a policy proposal that is so fact-based?

One of the best progressive speakers around today, John Edwards, provided a perfect example of how to do this in his 2004 Democratic Convention speech. In many respects, Edwards rivals Reagan in his ability to place the audience in a setting. Although his speech was not specifically about the minimum wage, the following section of the speech is a case study for progressives seeking to "set the stage" for a minimum wage proposal:

> I grew up in a small town in rural North Carolina, a place called Robbins. My father, he worked in a mill all his life, and I still remember vividly the men and women who worked in that mill with him. I can see them. Some of them had lint in their hair; some of them had grease on their faces. They worked hard, and they tried to put a little money away so that their kids and their grandkids could have a better life. The truth is, they're just like the auto workers, the office workers, the teachers and shop keepers on main streets all across this country.

> My mother had a number of jobs. She worked at the post office so she and my father could have health care. She owned her own small business. She refinished furniture to help pay for my education.

> I have had such incredible opportunities in my life. I was blessed to be the first person in my family to go to college.

I worked my way through, and I had opportunities beyond my wildest dreams.

And the heart of this campaign—your campaign, our campaign—is to make sure all Americans have exactly the same kind opportunities that I had no matter where you live, no matter who your family is, no matter what the color of your skin is.[3]

Edwards placed the audience on a very particular stage with a very particular set: the small town where he was raised, and the mill where his father worked. Edwards assembled a very particular cast on that set: the employees of the mill, covered with "grease on their faces." But then Edwards went one step further. After setting the stage with the mill, he gestured toward the auto plant, the post office, and his mother's furniture business—all similar sets with similar casts. This gesture gave these "small moments" the "big meaning" that defined his entire vision for a progressive presidential campaign: working to give all Americans the same opportunities that were given to him by the hard working people he grew up around.

We see in Edwards' words the same framing technique of setting the stage that Reagan used so effectively in his Farewell Speech, albeit to advance a diametrically opposed vision. Once the stage is set, the policy and the facts have a context, and the audience has an important frame of reference. At this point, the progressive politician can get more policy specific.

A progressive politician planning a speech on the minimum wage might take both Reagan and Edwards into account to set the stage along these lines:

Just the other day I was sitting at my kitchen table, thinking about how fortunate my life has been. Looking around me, I had everything I needed for a good life in America:

a beautiful family, a home full of love, a table with a warm meal. I work hard and every day when I come home I find all that I need. I felt lucky.

But there are millions of Americans who work hard at hourly jobs, then come home to find they are falling behind on their bills, they can barely afford the clothes their family needs and food to feed their children. When they look around they do not feel lucky. They feel stretched. They feel concerned.

Having set the stage, a progressive policy speech on the minimum wage can talk about the value to a community of keeping workers ahead of the cost of living, the importance of universal healthcare for a thriving economy, and the value of investment in worker training and education. But if the speaker overlooks the importance of first setting the stage, even the most viable policy proposals dangle in the air, then slip away. Setting the stage, in other words, is far more than narrative dressing: it is the essential act of grounding the frame in actual, lived experiences to create a bridge between the ideas and the listener.

[Activist]—Big Meaning, Small Things

The anti-war protest movement is one of the bedrock foundations of American progressive activism. In the 1960s and 1970s, the central progressive philosophy was that large-scale events involving hundreds of thousands of Americans was the best way to bring about political change. Indeed, the massive protests against the Vietnam War did have an impact on the policy decisions surrounding that war.

Today, in an age of increasingly sophisticated media-driven politics, large-scale protests do not seem to have the same impact they once had. Time and again, progressive activists have organized mass protests against the Iraq war. And while it is fair to say that these protests have had some impact in terms of galvanizing already involved progressive activists, they have not grown the anti-war movement substantially, nor have they had a huge impact on the policies of President Bush.

Recent progressive activists who have had a huge impact on America's view of the war have not taken a large-scale approach, but have focused on—as President Reagan said in his farewell speech—the "big meaning" in "small things." Consider, the inspiring success of Cindy Sheehan's 2005 "Camp Casey" protest. A year earlier, Sheehan's son, Army Specialist Casey Sheehan, had been killed in action in Iraq. In response to what she viewed as the injustice of the war, Sheehan headed to President Bush's ranch in Crawford, Texas to request a meeting with the President to discuss the death of her son and her view that the war must be stopped. President Bush responded by ignoring Sheehan's request for a meeting and denying her access to the ranch property. Sheehan subsequently pitched a tent by the side of the road near the ranch and continued to ask for a meeting with the President for the duration of his month-long vacation in Crawford.[4]

The impact of Sheehan's simple protest—a grieving mother in a tent a few miles from the President's summer ranch—far exceeded the media coverage and political impact of all other progressive protests since the invasion of Iraq. Sheehan became the voice and face of the progressive anti-war movement and her protest dramatically altered the balance of opinion about the war. It was the most significant progressive protest in American history since the 1963 Civil Rights March on Washington—and it involved only one person![5]

Why did Sheehan's protest succeed? Because it framed the injustice of the Iraq war in terms of "a small moment with a big meaning." Whereas progressive protests up to that point had framed the debate in terms of an immoral policy, Sheehan framed the debate in terms of her very real pain at the loss of her son. Her honest and focused expression of loss transformed the massive and impersonal anti-war movement into an intimate and personal event. As such, the iconic image of an anti-war protest as a city center filled with people was transformed into the image of a mother in anguish standing by the side of the road.

President Reagan was certainly not thinking of ways to make anti-war protests more effective when he spoke of "a small moment with a big meaning" in his farewell address. But the framing lesson in that speech turned out to be the perfect explanation for Sheehan's success.

Reagan's "small moment" frame and the success of Cindy Sheehan's protest suggest an entirely new paradigm for progressive activists in the age of media-driven politics: small protests that generate big meaning and lead to real change. Framing the debate, in other words, is not just about the words progressives choose to say, but also about the setting, the scale, and the focus of the actions they take. Framing a protest effectively—whether the focus of that protest is a war policy, the environment, or corporate corruption—involves critical thinking about small moments and the big meaning they can create in the eyes and ears of the American public.

[Citizen]—The Dinner Table

While President Reagan is often credited with articulating in speech the idea that "all great change begins at the dinner table," it is by no means an idea exclusive to him. Norman Rockwell's famous painting "Freedom From Want," which depicts a happy group of Americans around a dinner table set with a giant holiday turkey, also embodies this particular vision of America, perhaps better than any line in a presidential speech.

In terms of politics, however, the famous line from Reagan's Farewell Address articulates a very basic metaphor of:

[politics] is [people sitting at a table]

Rockwell and Reagan both invoked the frame of the dinner table as a place that defined the family, happiness, politics—the country itself. While progressives understand this basic principle, too often they downplay it, instead viewing the more impersonal public square as taking precedence as the foundation of the body politic. And to our great detriment, the Republican movement that has experienced such success over the past twenty years has taken advantage of this oversight.

For Republicans, the key to promoting a conservative vision of America has been transforming the dinner table—as well as the church pew—into places where "all great change begins." Despite the weaknesses in Republican ideology and the criminal and ethical scandals that have plagued the Republican party since the late 1990s, the conservative movement remains rooted in the belief that change and politics begins in the most basic of domestic places: home and church. For progressives to frame politics as a dinner table conversation is to take a giant step towards rooting a progressive vision within a broad conception of political participation connecting the family house to the White House.

Suggesting that we think about politics through the metaphor of "people at a table," however, does not mean that we should see every domestic moment as an opportunity for adversarial political debate. Rather, to frame politics in this way simply means to develop the habit and the skill to foster productive political debate in places and at moments where such debate is typically uncommon, such as mealtimes, carpools, coffee breaks, and gym workouts.

For example, the 2006 mid-term election saw a particularly fierce Senate campaign in Virginia between incumbent Senator George Allen and the Democratic challenger and eventual winner, Jim Webb. Over the course of the campaign, Allen was caught in a series of scandals in which his character came into question—first his use of a word with racist overtones ("macaca") and then his peculiar behavior surrounding revelations of his Jewish heritage. [6]

When the question of race comes up in politics, progressives are often unprepared to frame the debate. If the subject comes up in a conversation about an election campaign or in another context at the dinner table, progressives can seize upon the opportunity to foster a political debate in the following ways:

Ask "Why"—Ok, maybe he is a racist, maybe he isn't. But **why** do you think that word has generated so much interest?"

Ask "How"—"True . . . but isn't **how** he responded to the issue more important than his cultural heritage?"

Ask for "More"—"Well that's interesting. I've never thought of it that way. Can you tell me **more** about that?"

Ask to "Define"—"Well, that depends on what you mean by "politically correct"—**what** do you mean by it?"

The key to framing the dinner table as a place for political discussion is to steer potential confrontation into suggestive conversation. Too often, when politics come up, progressives (as well as conservatives) often leap directly to defending their side, which can have the effect of cutting off debate. To effectively frame a progressive issue, however, it is helpful to elicit, not cut off, the discussion—in other words, to foster the debate.

A good place to learn how to foster the debate is in the comment threads of progressive blogs. In a sense, these threads have become some of the most lively "dinner tables" in America over the last few years, and are ideal settings for developing the skill of fostering debate. Progressives can seek out contentious discussions and then enter into the comment threads with the specific goal of moderating the discussion rather than endorsing—or enforcing—a specific political position. And, since political debate on most blogs is much "louder" than most actual dinner table discussions, if you can foster a productive discussion online, fostering one at home should be easy.

15. GOVERNMENT IS A PERSON

BILL CLINTON, SECOND INAUGURAL (1997)[1]

Keywords: building, forward, future, journey, responsible

Strategy: Begin at the Beginning—Elevator Speech—Connect to Progressive Speakers

Quote

"When last we gathered, our march to this new future seemed less certain than it does today. We vowed then to set a clear course to renew our Nation. In these four years, we have been touched by tragedy, exhilarated by challenge, strengthened by achievement. America stands alone as the world's indispensable nation. Once again, our economy is the strongest on Earth. Once again, we are building stronger families, thriving communities, better educational opportunities, a cleaner environment. Problems that once seemed destined to deepen, now bend to our efforts. Our streets are safer, and record numbers of our fellow citizens have moved from welfare to work. And once again, we have resolved for our time a great debate over the role of Government. Today we can declare: Government is not the problem, and Government is not the solution. We—the American people—we are the solution. Our Founders understood that well and gave us a democracy strong enough to endure for centuries, flexible enough to face our common challenges and advance our common dreams in each new day. As times change, so Government must change. We need a new Government for a new century, humble enough not to try to solve all our problems for us but strong enough to give us the tools to solve our problems for ourselves, a government that is smaller, lives within its means, and does more with less. Yet where it can stand up for our values and interests around the world, and where it can give Americans the power to make a real difference in their everyday lives, Government should do more, not less. The preeminent mission of our new Government is to give all Americans an opportunity, not a guarantee but a real opportunity, to build better lives. Beyond that, my fellow citizens, the future is up to us. Our Founders taught us that the preservation of our liberty and our Union depends upon responsible citizenship. And we need a new sense of responsibility for a new century. There is work to do, work that Government alone cannot do: teaching children to read, hiring people off welfare rolls, coming out from behind locked doors and shuttered windows to help reclaim our streets from drugs and gangs and crime, taking time out of our own lives to serve others."

ANALYSIS

Bill Clinton was one of the most gifted public speakers of any President in recent times, displaying an ability to orate on a wide variety of topics with both eloquence and expertise. When he delivered his Second Inaugural Address on January 20, 1997, he displayed a masterful approach to framing the most complex and controversial subject any President could take on: government.

The theme of the speech had been developed over the course of his preceding reelection campaign, which was built around the theme that Clinton was the right person to help lead the nation across the "bridge to the 21st Century." Clinton had used that phrase in his stump speech, as well as in his 1996 acceptance speech to the Democratic Convention, where he repeated the word "bridge" twenty-six times.

The "bridge to the 21st century" is probably the most oft-cited and memorable phrase uttered by Clinton, and it served a very basic function during the 1996 campaign: to frame government programs. Clinton would begin his speech by talking about the "bridge" that we must build to reach the twenty-first century, and would follow that with a list of the government programs and changes he planned for his second term. Metaphorically, the logic was that America would "walk over" the "bridge" (e.g., programs) to reach the future. It was a simple and powerful metaphor.

What was most fascinating about President Clinton's Second Inaugural Speech, however, was that he hardly mentioned the word "bridge." He had established the "bridge" frame so strongly in his campaign that his audience understood it even though he only invoked it directly at the very end of the speech:

> Yes, let us build our bridge, a bridge wide enough and strong enough for every American to cross over to a blessed land of new promise.[2]

We see here the logic of government programs as something "strong" and "wide" for every American to "cross over." In Clinton's metaphor, government initiatives would give Americans the opportunity to walk from the twentieth to the twenty-first century. Each "century," accordingly, was defined metaphorically as one side of a canyon.

While Clinton framed government programs in his campaign, in his second inaugural he aimed much higher, to a broad frame for government itself. If we consider this passage, for example, an entirely new metaphor for government emerges:

> As times change, so Government must change. We need a new Government for a new century, humble enough not to try to solve all our problems for us but strong enough to give us the tools to solve our problems for ourselves, a government that is smaller, lives within its means, and does more with less.

Yet where it can stand up for our values and interests around the world, and where it can give Americans the power to make a real difference in their everyday lives, Government should do more, not less. The preeminent mission of our new Government is to give all Americans an opportunity, not a guarantee but a real opportunity, to build better lives.[3]

Given all these examples of what Clinton urged "government" to do and be in the speech, the logic of the frame was:

[government] is [a person]

At the heart of the speech was an attempt to frame government not as a large structure or system, but as a person. But not just any person: one who needed to change, to improve, almost as if government needed to enter a twelve-step program for over-spenders and underachievers in order to become more mature, humble and responsible in preparation for the challenges of the future.

Different from Jefferson's call for a "wise and frugal" government, Clinton advocated for both citizens and government to develop the same set of skills, the same ability to develop and provide opportunity, hence the frame, "Government is not the problem, and Government is not the solution." Government is instead a responsible person who, together with other responsible people, builds the bridge to the twenty-first century that we all, together, walk across.

Similar to Eisenhower, Johnson, and Carter, President Clinton also framed the idea of "progress" in terms of a split between material and non-material concerns. For Clinton, progress was "a nation ever moving forward towards realizing the full potential of all its citizens." In this respect, he framed progress as a journey down a path with significant obstacles. According to this logic, it was up to responsible citizens and a humble government to work together to overcome those obstacles.

Interestingly, while Clinton described material accomplishments in terms of achievement in his Second Inaugural Address—the material achievements of economic growth, reduced deficit spending, advancement in education and technology—he defined progress "in the human heart" as an ongoing challenge. At one point, he described Martin Luther King's vision of spiritual progress as "the ceaseless striving to live out our true creed," an idea that built on the frame of progress as a path full of obstacles that Americans overcome with the help of their government.

By invoking King in his Second Inaugural Address, Clinton set up one of the great big finishes of all presidential speeches. He had begun the speech with the frame of a "bridge" to the twenty-first century, moved to the idea of government as a humble person providing opportunity, and then pushed on to the idea of spiritual progress as the true work of a united America. To close, he wrapped this entire package in a vision of the American dream:

> May those generations whose faces we cannot yet see, whose names we may never know, say of us here that we led our beloved land into a new century with the American dream alive for all her children, with the American promise of a more perfect Union a reality for all her people, with America's bright flame of freedom spreading throughout all the world. From the height of this place and the summit of this century, let us go forth.[4]

With those lines, President Clinton repackaged his entire argument in a biblical refrain consistent with King's vision of a "promised land."[5] The end of the twentieth century that Clinton spoke of during his campaign for reelection became "the summit" on which a unified American people stood posed to march forward, "bright flame of freedom" in hand. His vision for America became an image of the country not only framed through key metaphors of the path and the bridge, but also rooted in an American voice from recent history.

As an example of framing core issues in American political

debate, few presidential speeches are more accomplished than Bill Clinton's Second Inaugural Address.

STRATEGY

[Politician]—Begin At The Beginning

On a basic level, most progressive speeches begin by discussing situations that lack something or are in need of repair, then prescribing how we can work toward building something better. In other words, progressives talk about *moving forward*. Conservatives, by contrast, usually start their speeches by talking about breaking apart something that they view as a hindrance to achievement. In other words, conservatives talk about *moving backwards*.

With an eye towards finding the best way to frame the start of a progressive speech, candidates and elected officials should consider the opening lines of President Clinton's Second Inaugural, which has one of the clearest progressive beginnings of any speech:

> My fellow citizens, at this last Presidential Inauguration of the 20th century, let us lift our eyes toward the challenges that await us in the next century. It is our great good fortune that time and chance have put us not only at the edge of a new century, in a new millennium, but on the edge of a bright new prospect in human affairs, a moment that will define our course and our character for decades to comes. We must keep our old democracy forever young. Guided by the ancient vision of a promised land, let us set our sights upon a land of new promise.[6]

In Clinton's frame, "beginning" is defined as the "edge of a new century." This definition evoked the image of Americans standing before the "edge" of a cliff looking forward—the progressive ideal of looking to the promise of the future while still aware of the obstacles to be overcome in the present.

As Clinton showed, a good beginning orients the listener and clearly establishes the point from which the candidate will move forward—where his or her vision will take us. To define a beginning, a politician must answer three basic questions:

- Where are we now?
- Where are we heading?
- Are there obstacles ahead?

Thinking in these terms forces a progressive candidate to orient and establish their vision. In a discussion of education, for example, a speech might begin along these lines:

> The challenge ahead of us is not just to build better schools, but to create the best schools in the world. Today, we stand at the beginning of that journey, looking ahead to smaller classrooms, more teachers, better technology, and state of the art curricula to prepare America's kids for the challenges of tomorrow. But to get there, we must find our way past obstacles that threaten to stop us in our tracks: insufficient training, funding, and willpower. Our future depends on getting past these obstacles together.

This kind of beginning, drawing on the basic logic of President Clinton's Second Inaugural, invites the listener to join in the candidate's vision, and sets up the later discussion of policy.

[Activist]—Elevator Speech

One of the most important tools a progressive activist needs is an "elevator speech," a short, one sentence statement that explains what it means to be a progressive. Elevator speeches are actually an old sales technique, and sales teams have them on hand at all times in case they find themselves with a new prospect and not enough time to get out a full pitch.

According to *The American Prospect,* this is what the Republican elevator speech has been for the past few years:

We believe in freedom and liberty, low taxes, less government, traditional values, and a strong defense.[7]

A basic formula for an elevator speech can be gleaned from this example. It starts with a clear statement of belief ("We believe in") followed by an enunciation of the two most prominent core values of the party ("freedom and liberty") followed by a mix of issues and metaphors that express core values ("lower taxes, less government, traditional values, strong defense.") The formula can be defined as:

[Statement of belief] in [value] and [value], [expressed value], [expressed value], and [expressed value].

In terms of teaching activists to "sell" a progressive vision, the elevator speech is a powerful tool because it brings us up to the highest possible level in the discussion: the level of values. All political debate exists on three levels: values (top), issues (middle), and policy (bottom).[8] Progressives love to talk on the bottom two levels because they seem more "real" and concrete. Policy and issues are where the facts are. You can put policy onto paper and make an issue a web page heading. Values are tougher to figure out.

One way to create an elevator speech is to actually build one step by step by first picking two of these progressive values and swapping them into our formula:

Community	Equality	Strength	Fairness
Cooperation	Honesty	Unity	Security
Fulfillment	Prosperity	Service	Progress
Responsibility	Protection	Opportunity	Empathy[9]

Clearly, these are not the only progressive values that exist, but this is a good list to start from. Having picked two—progress and opportunity, we now have the beginnings of an elevator speech that looks like this:

We believe in [progress] and [opportunity]

Next, we need to pick three or four "expressed value" statements to back up our core beliefs. To build an expressed value is easy. Try starting with another basic value, such as "protection," and, rather than just stating it, turn it into a metaphor: [protection] is [a community]. Hillary Clinton's famous phrase "it takes a village" is an expression of the [protection] is [a community] metaphor. Another expression that follows logically is "strong communities," which I happen to like, as it's short, quick and gets the point across.[10] Add two more expressed values to our formula and our elevator speech looks like this:

We believe in [prosperity] and [opportunity], [strong communities], [healthy families] and [the world's best schools].

Based on this formula, we can see how this line from President Clinton's Second Inaugural is a good example of a progressive elevator speech:

Once again, we are building stronger families, thriving communities, better educational opportunities, a cleaner environment

While elevator speeches will differ based on the needs of an individual organization, negotiating the structure of one is a great way to build unity. Once the elevator speech has been constructed, it can be printed on cards, memorized and used in the field. And, as it frames the discussion with a clear statement of values, every political encounter becomes an opportunity to use the elevator speech. When we move up to the level of values, our ideas will be clearer to us and to others, and our responses will be stronger and hit harder.

[Citizen]—Connect To Progressive Speakers

Over the last several years, the Republican movement has flooded the public debate with so much rhetoric that many progressives have become wholly consumed with merely responding and have, as a result, lost touch with the broader tradition of progressive thinkers and speakers. But, one of the most powerful and important resources that progressives have are the long tradition of American voices that have come before them, a legacy that grounds contemporary progressive speech in the thread of ideas dating back to the Constitution. To connect the current debate to past progressive speakers, we need only mention them.

In his Second Inaugural, President Clinton framed his ideas within the broader tradition of progressive ideas by connecting his speech to another delivered three decades before:

> Thirty-four years ago, the man whose life we celebrate today spoke to us down there, at the other end of this Mall, in words that moved the conscience of a nation. Like a prophet of old, he told of his dream that one day America would rise up and treat all its citizens as equals before the law and in the heart. Martin Luther King's dream was the American dream. His quest is our quest: the ceaseless striving to live out our true creed. Our history has been built on such dreams and labors. And by our dreams and labors, we will redeem the promise of America in the 21st century.[11]

As I mentioned earlier in the analysis of the speech, the framing choice President Clinton made was to close his Second Inaugural Address with a discussion of the American Dream, which invoked the logic of Martin Luther King's 1963 "I Have A Dream" speech.[12] This was not just a call for material success, but a call for unity in the face of "petty bickering," and a call to "the ceaseless striving to live out our true creed."

While not all efforts to connect the debate to previous progressive speeches need be as grand as that by President Clinton, connecting to past progressive speakers is just as important in a dinner table conversation as it is in an inaugural address. The ability to connect a conversation to other great progressive speakers is the product of these factors:

Familiarity: An active awareness of past progressive speakers and their speeches

Habit: Thinking about the current debate in terms of progressive ideas that came before

Practice: Trying repeatedly to connect current ideas with the words of prior speakers

Signposting: Key phrases inserted into the debate that direct people to the words of past progressive speakers.

Familiarity, habit and practice each take some time to pick up, but signposts are relatively easy to learn. For example, the next time the subject of politics comes up at the dinner table, progressives might try one of these signposts:

- This whole discussion about education **reminds me** of Johnson's Great Society speech.
- Eisenhower **once said** that the key to sound foreign policy was that all powers, strong and weak, should come to the table.
- The person **who said this best**, I think, was Jefferson when he described a "wise and frugal government" as the key to the American system.
- **This is exactly what** Teddy Roosevelt **meant** when he said

that muckraking without ethics would lead to cynicism towards government.

- **I can almost hear** Kennedy's voice as we have this discussion.

Each of these phrases directs the listener to a key moment in the history of progressive speechmaking, and brings to the table, as it were, an important voice in the conversation. And, when we connect the current conversation to previous speakers, the debate begins to move beyond emotional reactions toward a far-reaching progressive vision.

16. EVIL WILL ATTACK

GEORGE W. BUSH—STATE OF THE UNION (2002)[1]

Keywords: doomsday, either-or, repetition, selling, terror

Strategy: Ticking Bomb—Magic Words—Turning on the Lights

Quote

"States like these, and their terrorist allies, constitute an axis of evil, arming to threaten the peace of the world. By seeking weapons of mass destruction, these regimes pose a grave and growing danger. They could provide these arms to terrorists, giving them the means to match their hatred. They could attack our allies or attempt to blackmail the United States. In any of these cases, the price of indifference would be catastrophic. We will work closely with our coalition to deny terrorists and their state sponsors the materials, technology, and expertise to make and deliver weapons of mass destruction. We will develop and deploy effective missile defenses to protect America and our allies from sudden attack. And all nations should know: America will do what is necessary to ensure our nation's security. We'll be deliberate, yet time is not on our side. I will not wait on events, while dangers gather. I will not stand by, as peril draws closer and closer. The United States of America will not permit the world's most dangerous regimes to threaten us with the world's most destructive weapons. Our war on terror is well begun, but it is only begun. This campaign may not be finished on our watch—yet it must be and it will be waged on our watch. We can't stop short. If we stop now—leaving terror camps intact and terror states unchecked—our sense of security would be false and temporary. History has called America and our allies to action, and it is both our responsibility and our privilege to fight freedom's fight. Our first priority must always be the security of our nation, and that will be reflected in the budget I send to Congress. My budget supports three great goals for America: We will win this war; we'll protect our homeland; and we will revive our economy."

ANALYSIS

For all the emphasis on ideas and metaphors, one of the most important framing techniques used in recent American politics is repetition. The simple act of repeating the same keywords over and over again in a speech has been a hallmark of a certain kind of framing associated with the team of communications experts who propelled George Bush to the presidency in 2000 and again in 2004. The public relations firm associated with Frank Luntz, for example, has spent millions of dollars using quasi-scientific techniques to determine which magic words elicit the proper responses when repeated by Republicans. The end result has been a Republican framing style that falls somewhere between the monotonous repetition of a jingoistic drumbeat and the empty rhetoric of a used car dealership commercial. Once the keywords for the month are set in place in the media and reinforced endlessly by high-placed Republican political figures, they hold the frame in place.

To date in the history of presidential speeches, the grand master of repetition as a technique of political framing has been President George W. Bush. While it has been routine for pundits to criticize Bush's studied "down home" diction and twisted neologisms, these criticisms often overlook his unrivaled gift for repetition. Far beyond the cliché of "staying on message," Bush has established core ideas and key logical frameworks in the American mind—almost always to the detriment of the public good.

Nowhere was President Bush's use of repetition as a framing technique more apparent than in the State of the Union Address he delivered on January 29, 2002—the so-called "Axis of Evil" speech. The focus of the speech was the "war on terror"—the oft-repeated phrase that has since become a general rubric for a vast array of foreign and domestic policies. In the speech, Bush framed what he saw as a fight against terrorism in terms of "evil":

> States like these, and their terrorist allies, constitute an axis
> of evil, arming to threaten the peace of the world.

The phrase "axis of evil" described a group of nations that included Afghanistan, Iraq, Iran, North Korea, Syria, Libya, Lebanon, and Somalia. What made them "evil" in President Bush's logic was a radical idea that not only alarmed an entire segment of the American public, but set the United States on course towards a disastrous preemptive strike military policy. "Evil" nations, as President Bush defined them, were not just those nations that posed a current and direct threat to the United States, but also those nations that "could" pose a threat in the future by providing resources, arms or refuge for terrorists groups. The logic looked something like this:

> [evil] is [potential direct or indirect future danger]

There is considerable question, however, as to whether President Bush was truly interested in defining evil in his speech or whether his goal was to focus public debate on the fear evoked through a repetition of keywords related to evil. In framing the "war on terror," in other words, Bush focused more on heightened panic through repetition than on clarifying key concepts. Consider the number of times each of the following keywords or their derivatives were repeated in the 48-minute speech:

terror (terrorism, terrorists, etc.) x 36
security (secure, securing, etc.) x 20
war (war on terror, etc.) x 16
weapons (of mass destruction, etc.) x 12
danger (dangerous, etc.) x 8
enemy (enemies, etc.) x 6
evil x 5100 [3]

The sheer quantity of these repeated keywords made President Bush's State of the Union Address more of an exercise in mental conditioning than a policy speech. The pounding repetition of words connoting danger was, in fact, designed to establish in the public's mind the basic logic that would soon thereafter convince the country, and the Congress, of the falsely claimed need to invade and occupy Iraq.

Beyond the repetition of these words, Bush's speech also used the so-called "doomsday scenario" as a technique of narrative framing. The following year, when Bush and Vice President Cheney began their bid for reelection to a second term, the doomsday scenario became the dominant framing technique in their stump speeches. In the 2002 State of the Union Address, the doomsday scenario, while a minor tactic, was still quite potent.

President Bush's doomsday scenario consisted of telling the American public a very simple story of the horrific destruction that would befall the country if it elected to follow policies other than the ones that he proposed. The logic was a simple zero sum of "follow me and live" or "follow the Democrats and die." In the State of the Union speech, the doomsday story involved weapons of mass destruction being used on American soil—in other words, Armageddon being unleashed upon the United States:

By seeking weapons of mass destruction, these regimes

pose a grave and growing danger. They could provide these arms to terrorists, giving them the means to match their hatred. They could attack our allies or attempt to blackmail the United States. In any of these cases, the price of indifference would be catastrophic. We will work closely with our coalition to deny terrorists and their state sponsors the materials, technology, and expertise to make and deliver weapons of mass destruction.[4]

In the months and years following President Bush's 2002 State of the Union Address, the louder the critique of his policies grew, the more horrific the details of the doomsday scenario became. The doomsday scenario, in other words, with all its grim images of weapons being used against the American people by evil terrorists, was essentially Bush's variation on a very simple idea: "vote for me."

The logic of the doomsday story is far more sinister and, unfortunately, far more effective than the mere details it puts forward. This is because the doomsday story traps the listener in an "either-or" frame—a zero sum game with no room for compromise:

[Either: support my policies] vs. [Or: America will be destroyed by terrorists]

Either "A" or "B" is the logic of the frame—and there are never any middle ground positions. When we think about President Bush's demeanor in general, his entire outlook is grounded in this "either-or" frame. All nations were "either" with us "or" against us. And the consequences of that choice was "either" war "or" peace.

Once extended, the "either-or" frame results in an endless series of falsely stark choices. To invade or not to invade, to cancel a program or not to cancel, to kill or not to kill. In the intolerant atmosphere of the "either-or" frame, the basic stuff of government itself—compromise— is banished. All choices are urgent. All decisions are final. All political actors are either the closest of friends or the harshest of enemies.

The most extreme version of this "either-or" logic came during the debate in the House and Senate over the 2006 Military Commissions Act that ultimately gave President Bush the authority to name anyone he deemed to have connections to terrorism an "enemy combatant," to deny that "enemy combatant" the writ of habeas corpus, and to permit interrogation techniques that both international law and the U.S. military recognized as torture.[5] In his statements and speeches in support of those measures, Bush accused critics wanting to wait for terrorists to attack the United States before acting to protect the country.[6] In other words, either Americans supported the President's desire to imprison and torture whomever he pleased, or America would be destroyed by terrorists.

Despite all the horrific scenarios that the President and his staff unleashed on the American public between 2004 and 2007, it was in the relative political calm of the State of the Union Address in 2002 where he first set the "either-or" frame, which would become the dominant framing technique of his entire presidency. Under the guise of reporting on the state of the nation, Bush used the basic technique of repetition to trap political debate in a crippling and dangerous "either-or" logic.

STRATEGY

[Politician]—Ticking Bomb

The frame that has dominated the debate on torture during the presidency of George W. Bush is the "ticking bomb" scenario:

> The police discover that a terrorist cell plans to blow up the city with a bomb, which is set to explode in one hour. Suddenly, the police capture a known terrorist. Upon initial questioning, the prisoner reveals nothing of the plot. So, in order to find out where the bomb is located and disarm it, thereby saving millions of lives, the police decide to torture the prisoner to extract information.[7]

As the 2002 State of the Union Address showed, one of the key tactics that President Bush has used to dominate debate—and particularly the debate on national security—is the "either-or" logic invoked by the doomsday scenario. This same logic is at work in the "ticking bomb" frame.

The first major premise of the "ticking bomb" scenario is how it frames the idea of "knowledge" or "information." Applied to the torture narrative, it frames the need to get knowledge "out of" someone, i.e., the suspected terrorist. When someone is tortured, people often talk about "breaking" the person, or doing what is necessary to get them to "reveal what they know." This is a metaphor of "knowledge" as a thing that is inside of someone. Once this idea of knowledge or information is established, the rest follows.

Torture, in this conception, is identical to the "break glass in case of emergency" sign we see in many buildings, usually with a large axe behind the glass. Under normal circumstances, we would never break the glass, take out the axe and start hacking at people's doors. However, if there is an emergency, like a fire in the building, the normal rules of "do not break public property" no longer apply, and it is okay to break the glass in order to save lives.

In the case of the "ticking bomb" scenario, the axe is the knowledge or information "inside" the terrorist. Ordinarily, we would not break the glass. But when there is a "fire" (e.g., a nuclear bomb hidden in the middle of a city) we have a moral imperative to break the glass to get the "axe" out.

The problem, of course, with this idea is that President Bush's larger argument about the "war on terror" puts no definitions or limits on which buildings are burning and how many prisoners must be broken. The definition and urgency of a specific danger—and the means to break the prisoner—are put entirely in the hands of the President. And in that situation, the choice to torture not only violates human rights, but all rights of citizenship as defined in the constitution.

To reframe the "ticking bomb" scenario, progressive candidates and politicians might begin by asking this basic question:

Why have we failed to outsmart and out-hustle the terrorists?

This helps us to see the basic structure of a completely new way of talking about national security that defines torture as a security failure, not an act of strength. From here flows a new scenario for national security for progressive candidates, one where America never depends on a suspect to confess where the "ticking bomb" is hidden. In this new scenario, security will have failed if we have not worked hard enough, fast enough and—most importantly—smart enough to anticipate and prevent the "ticking bomb" from being hidden in the first place.

Under this new scenario, when we capture the suspect, we still want to place him or her in a secure room, but, from that point forward, a radically different progressive logic emerges. With the prisoner in a room, it is now the American security forces that tell the prisoner something he or she did not know when they arrived there: "We found the bomb before your colleague placed it, now let's talk." Security results from outsmarting and out-hustling the enemy.

Let us return to the "ticking bomb" scenario and now look at it from the perspective of the "outsmart and out-hustle" frame. With this frame in place, the police or military interrogator are no longer the embodiment of power and strength, but the very image of the dumb brute. And the terrorist is not the embodiment of mortal danger, but instead the smiling, clever crook. The scene in the interrogation room—the place where the "ticking bomb" frame asks us to suspend our morals to allow for torture—is now framed as the classic encounter between the angry and frustrated dumb brute, and the silent and smug genius criminal. By embracing and repeating the "ticking bomb" scenario, progressives inadvertently accept the image of America as that dumb brute, unable to solve problems, unable to anticipate. This new frame, however, can help progressive candidates and politicians craft statements such as:

- "Rather than trying to outsmart and out-hustle the threats to America, the Republicans under President Bush took the road to failure by trying to protect America with the tactics of the dumb brute."
- "Every child in America knows, it is Jack who outsmarts the giant, and it is David who slays Goliath. The dumb brute may look menacing in the short run, but he is always brought down by someone smarter."
- "America can no longer afford to let the failed tactics of the Bush White House drag the nation into failure after failure using the dangerous tactics of the dumb brute."

Ultimately, altering the scenario that has kept torture in place as the Republican policy of choice accomplishes much more than just a change in the content of the debate. By reframing torture, progressive candidates can do a better job protecting America. After all, to keep America safe, we must outsmart and out-hustle those who seek to do us harm.

[Activist]—Magic Words

President Bush's 2002 State of the Union Address demonstrated the central place that repetition of keywords played in framing the debate to advance a particular vision of preemptive military strikes, unchecked executive power, and torture. It follows logically, therefore, that unwittingly repeating these keywords would also help to reinforce that frame. Accordingly, identifying and alerting others to the keywords in a debate—the "magic words" that frame problematic policies or ideas—can be an essential role for progressive activists to play.

Finding problematic "magic words" so as to avoid repeating them is a skill progressive activists can quickly pick up. The key is to switch from reading to processing the media. Most people wait for political debate to come to them through broadcast or print media, and then react to the ideas presented. In order to be able to spot politically charged "magic words," progressives must become more active at building their own sources for political debate—of finding and comparing various aspects of the debate as it unfolds in the media.

For example, while all of Bush's speeches are discussed in the news media, they are also made available in full on the White House website (www.whitehouse.gov). To spot the magic words in one of Bush's speeches, activists can begin by reading the transcript, and circling significant words that he repeats over and over again.

In conjunction with that, progressives must figure out which repeated words are "magic words" and which are not. To determine which words are repeated in order to hold in place the debate, progressives can check the scripts on the White House website against news coverage and other organizations or think tanks politically aligned with Bush. For example, to spot Bush's "magic words," a progressive might quickly read a few blogs, *Yahoo* news, the *Washington Post*, *Fox News*, and perhaps take a look at the website for the conservative think tank The Heritage Foundation. This initial skim will help to see if any magic words from the recent postings on the White House website are popping up in other places.

Next, progressive activists can analyze how the particular magic words identified are working—i.e., what bigger ideas do they invoke and how? This analysis seems tricky at first but it gets easier with each attempt.

Finally—and this is a crucial step—progressive activists need to post their analysis of the "magic words" in a prominent place, such as a blog, in order to warn others about them. Whenever new "magic words" are communicated by the White House or other conservative organizations, it is imperative for progressive activists to get the word out about them to other activists so they do not fall into the trap of repeating them.

[Citizen]—Turning on the Lights

Spreading the fear of America being attacked by a single bomb or weapon that can kill thousands of people is not a new rhetorical strategy. However, reframing the fear-laden debate is something that progressive citizens are just beginning to tackle. For example, in a dinner table conversation, a friend or family member might express their deep fear in this way:

- "We have to keep fighting them because these people want to kill us!"
- "Anyone could bring a bomb into the country and blow us all up!"
- "I worry that if we don't kill the terrorists first, their next attack will be even worse!"

These kinds of statements, which most progressives have overheard in one form or another, are troubling because they trap the debate in a "fear" frame. Once the specter of an attack is unleashed rhetorically, it is particularly difficult to move the discussion forward. For example, one might say that more people die each year from coronary heart disease than from terrorist attacks—or one might say that drunk driving accidents cause more deaths per year than all the deaths on September 11, 2001, combined, but facts such as these never seem to move the debate back to a reasonable discussion of the type of threat that terrorism poses. How, then, can progressives liberate the debate from the fear frame?

In an era when Republicans ran campaign ads showing mushroom clouds, where President Bush and Vice President Cheney both consistently told the American people that they would suffer deadly attacks if Democrats were elected, reframing the debate could begin by posing this simple question:

Why do Republicans talk about terrorist attacks the most when Democrats are leading in an election or in opinion polls?

The strategy is to focus attention on the politics of the fear, and to refocus attention from the fear to the Republican politics behind it. The key to this strategy is to picture people trapped in the fear frame as similar to people sitting in a dark cinema watching a horror movie. After a while, the audience becomes so enthralled with the movie that they forget they are sitting in a theater and begin to react to the horror scenes as if they are real. Reframing, in this instance, is the equivalent of standing up and turning on the lights. Suddenly, everyone has a chance to see that they are watching a movie—or a political advertisement—and that the fear is more a product of what they are watching than the danger itself.

In the 2006 midterm elections, the Republican National Committee ran an ad they called "Stakes."[8] This ad was constructed like a horror film and was designed to trap viewers in the fear frame, employing a doomsday logic to convince the public that a vote for a Democratic Party candidate would result in a nuclear attack on the United States by Al Qaeda or Iran. If a political ad such as this one came up in conversation, progressives could "turn on the lights" by drawing attention to the campaign politics behind the fear frame, and then lead an honest discussion about smart security, strong leadership and a secure future.

In the end, fear does not always dissipate under the lights of reframing. Persistent fear framing, as has been the case under President Bush's administration, can etch emotions deep into the political habits of citizens, and reframing the politics behind the use of the fear frame may not bring an end to everyone's anxieties. But persistent refusal to accept the fear frame can foster productive discussion of the dangers we face, as opposed to perpetuating political accusations against progressives. And once the fear begins to recede, meaningful dinner table conversations about protecting and securing America can flourish.

17. THE THREE P'S OF PROGRESSIVE POLITICS

Politics at its most basic is made up not of words or speeches, but of habits. Consider, for example, the following scenario that unfolds in millions of homes each day:

> *7:00 a.m., Anytown, USA*—A woman turns on the television to listen to the news while preparing her breakfast. Cup of coffee in hand, she overhears the anchor say, ". . . and in his most recent speech, the President said that Democrats voted against legislation designed to protect Americans from terrorism . . ."

When approached through a familiar set of habits—the old experience of progressive politics—this moment is no different from any other moment. The words are just part of a newscast, a summary of events that may be factually questionable, but are not necessarily politically significant. The listener turns back to making breakfast, drinks her coffee, and begins the day without incident.

But approached through a new set of habits—the experience of framing the debate—the scenario changes dramatically. Now, while listening to the announcer, several keywords leap out at our "progressive framer":

- "protect"
- "terrorism"
- "voted against"

With coffee cup in hand and these three words in her mind, our progressive framer flips open her laptop and brings up the local newspaper. Exactly as she suspected: these words appear in two articles. She immediately goes to the White House website to skim transcripts of the President's recent speeches. As she reads over the first few lines of the President's last radio address, she notices the word "protect" and "terrorism" repeated over and over again. At the same time that she is doing this, an email update from a progressive blog shows up in her inbox announcing that casualty rates are up in Al Anbar Province in Iraq.

Her cup of coffee now finished, our progressive framer grabs her keys and heads out the door for the commute to work, a set of questions now running through her mind:

- Who is making this claim?
- How are the words "protect" and "terrorism" being used?
- What is the unspoken logic being driven by this statement?
- Which words will I use to reframe this idea?

As this example shows, framing the debate is not just about finding that one campaign slogan or about crafting the perfect political ad—it is a set of habits that structures a new experience of politics. It is ongoing, daily, and long-term, and involves three key concepts—participation, principle and promise.

Participation—"Bottom Up" vs. "Top Down"
Over the past twenty years, the Republicans have advanced a vast effort to frame the debate in "conservative" terms through the use

of a hierarchical or "top down" approach. The cycle begins when Washington, D.C. based political communications agencies are asked by the Republican National Committee to generate lists of keywords and key phrases. These lists are distributed to elected Republicans in Congress, Republican figures in the media, Republican think tanks, and leadership in the Republican political base—with instructions to all these groups to repeat the "approved" terms. Eventually, President Bush gives a speech using the distributed keywords and the entire Republican leadership echoes in unison as the terms of the debate unfold in perfect step across the American political culture.

This "top down" model results in the frustrating, intolerant absolutism that permeates every corner of Republican politics. Turn on any talk show with a Republican slant, and you will hear the keywords repeated. Ask a Republican friend their view of the current issue, and you will hear them repeat the keywords. Ironically, while the Republican Party dreams of dismantling any semblance of a centralized Federal government save for a standing army, their entire vision of framing is based on a strong centralized, top down approach. The bottom of the party repeats the keywords that the top chooses for them, and they keep repeating them until any pretense of an actual exchange of ideas has been suffocated.

Progressive framing takes a vastly different "bottom up" approach, which encourages participation, not blind obedience. Progressive attempts at framing the debate begin with the discussion of a particular issue, which generates comments or short essays which then circulate through the vast social network of email lists, websites, and organizations that make up the progressive grassroots infrastructure.

Both pushed on and drawn outward at the same time, the framing discussion eventually flows into the in-boxes and briefing notes of political staffers, as well as to the reading lists of non-activists. Simultaneously, progressive efforts to frame a particular issue "break through" to the much broader discussion unfolding in the print and broadcast news. Eventually, elected officials and candidates craft messages influenced by the initial progressive framing efforts, and a core frame begins to emerge.

The "bottom up" approach to progressive framing results in a staggering level of participation in political debate from the grassroots up to the highest levels of media and government. The result is not a single, monotonous repetition of keywords picked by a party elite, but a debate about a progressive vision that citizens, activists, media figures, and political leaders all participate in.

"Top down" versus "bottom up" participation in framing the debate is also different not just for the flow of ideas it produces, but for the impact it has on political culture in America. "Bottom up" progressive framing nourishes a healthy American political culture filled with more voices and more points of view, whereas "top down" conservative framing chokes off political participation, and gives control of the debate to an increasingly small, increasingly deceptive—and increasingly divisive—ruling elite.

Principle

While participation is the most tangible and immediate result of progressive efforts at framing the debate, it is only one part of the bright constellation of principles that constitute progressivism, which can be understood in reference to these basic questions:

- What is good government?
- What do Americans hope to achieve for themselves?
- How should America relate to other nations?
- What will the legacy of America be?

Since George Washington's time, good government has been framed in terms of the inclusion of—as opposed to the rule over—the people. This principle has been presented in a variety of ways, but the broad logic of "We the People" has always endured. But rarely discussed is the intrinsic progressive logic to the "We the People" frame of good government. "We the People," in other words, is the principle out of which the ideal is formed. Abraham Lincoln articulated it best:

government of the people, by the people, for the people[1]

In Lincoln's frame, the earth does not tip naturally towards the ideals of equal justice and representation, but is driven toward it by dedication to the American principle of good government. "We the People," in other words, pushes against the continuing tension in America between the tendency for power and wealth to accumulate in the hands of the few, and the progressive attempt to counterbalance that accumulation. "Good government," in a progressive vision emerges, in other words, as a force for restoring the underlying principle of "We the People" when that principle has been betrayed by force or by failure. For progressives, "bad government" is based on inequality and justice for the few, while good government fosters justice equally for everyone.

The principle of a just government is not just an abstract progressive philosophy, but has as its goal the creation of the conditions that all Americans need in order to achieve a better future. Jimmy Carter stated this principle most directly:

Confidence has defined our course and has served as a link between generations. We've always believed in something called progress. We've always had faith that the days of our children would be better than our own.[2]

The best way to achieve a better future for our children and ourselves has long been a subject of debate between two competing forces of progressive achievement: the material and the spiritual. Both Theodore Roosevelt and Lyndon Johnson framed crisis points in American history in terms of the failure of Americans to attain their material needs, which in turn stifled the nations ability to achieve its broader, spiritual needs.[3] The Great Society, in other words, is a towering structure of spiritual progress built on an ever-expanding foundation of material improvement.

Just as it articulates the principles of inclusive government and a better future for every American, a progressive vision also defines the basic principles by which America relates to other nations, that of peace and law. Both Woodrow Wilson and Harry Truman stated that the true enemies of America were not other nations, but any "false philosophy" that sought to dominate the "free highways of the world."[4] Ironically, however, it was Republican Dwight Eisenhower who presented the clearest, most articulate progressive vision for American foreign policy:

> We face a hostile ideology—global in scope, atheistic in character, ruthless in purpose, and insidious in method. Unhappily the danger it poses promises to be of indefinite duration. To meet it successfully, there is called for, not so much the emotional and transitory sacrifices of crisis, but rather those which enable us to carry forward steadily, surely, and without complaint the burdens of a prolonged and complex struggle—with liberty at stake. Only thus shall we remain, despite every provocation, on our charted course toward permanent peace and human betterment.[5]

The progressive principles of foreign relations are not served, in other words, by rallying the people to the panic of war, but by leading the country through the long course to a permanent peace. As John Kennedy emphasized, charting this course means that while no enemy should be tempted by American weakness, neither can we depend on what he called an "uncertain balance of terror." Peace in a progressive vision is achieved not through fear or destruction, but through law, diplomacy, agreement, and mutual recognition. In a progressive vision, America is protected by its moral, economic and military strength. But the country achieves peace, ultimately, only when it is willing to sit down for balanced and equal discussion at the negotiating table. When our leaders refuse to sit down at the table for fear of the appearance of acquiescence or weakness, both peace and security quickly dissipate.

Thus, the legacy of America, as envisioned by the progressive movement, rests neither in conquest nor power, but in the most perishable of all human circumstances: opportunity for all. For John Kennedy and Bill Clinton alike, the challenge America constantly faced was to find the will to achieve, the resolve to seize hold of the opportunity presented with such abundance—the opportunity, as they put it metaphorically, to build a bridge to the future or to reach the stars.[6] It was Franklin Roosevelt who best articulated this progressive vision of the legacy of America when he spoke to the nation in the heart of the Great Depression:

> If I read the temper of our people correctly, we now realize as we have never realized before our interdependence on each other; that we can not merely take but we must give as well; that if we are to go forward, we must move as a trained and loyal army willing to sacrifice for the good of a common discipline, because without such discipline no progress is made, no leadership becomes effective. We are, I know, ready and willing to submit our lives and property to such discipline, because it makes possible a leadership which aims at a larger good. This I propose to offer, pledging that the larger purposes will bind upon us all as a sacred obligation with a unity of duty hitherto evoked only in time of armed strife.[7]

What we see in Roosevelt's words is that whenever opportunity for all is in jeopardy, the progressive voice calls for unity and shared sacrifice. Roosevelt framed his efforts in military logic not because progressivism is a violent vision, but because progressivism demands the dedication and sacrifice of those seeking to overcome obstacles to equality and opportunity. Poverty, racism, fascism—each in their own time have threatened to eliminate the primary legacy of American opportunity for all, and each in turn was faced down by unity, shared sacrifice, and dedicated might. Indeed, the greatest moments in America's collective imagination has been when citizens came together to eliminate the threats to equality of opportunity.

Promise

For several decades now, the conservative movement has promised the following "results" to people who voted for its candidates:

- Material wealth
- Military protection
- Control over cultural values

These "results" have been guaranteed through a series of measures that conservatives promised to enact once they were in office, such as:

- Tax refunds, market deregulation, and union busting
- Weapons spending, military expansion, and preemptive strikes
- Promotion of religion, and prohibition of certain behavior

In the end, however, those who benefited from the conservative promise were a much smaller group than those who initially believed in it. The promise that resulted in Republican control of all three branches of government, in other words, revealed itself to bring about, instead of the above promises, the following *actual* results:

- Concentration of wealth
- Irresponsible use of the military
- Cultural divisiveness

What, then, is the progressive promise? Three key results are paramount, all of which are rooted in the history of a progressive vision and speak to the urgencies of contemporary America:

- Responsible government
- Opportunity for everyone
- Smart security

The progressive promise frames American politics in terms of a vision of responsibility, opportunity, and security to be codified in a core set of measures:

- Protecting Americans through honest and active diplomacy, a firm policy of guarding all the gates into the country, and a shift towards independence from foreign nations for vital sources of energy.
- To advance opportunity for everyone through universal healthcare, great public schools for all children, and fair wages.
- To return confidence in government through fair elections, balanced and accountable representation of the people, and equal rights for all citizens.

Each of these measures indicate not only the new results a progressive promise will bring, but also what is wrong with the policies currently in place. But, while reframing initially takes the form of a response to current flawed policies, critique is not the purpose of advancing a progressive promise. Instead, the goal is to move the debate to a new logic, which affords a new ability to see how and why flawed policies have failed, as well as a new ability to craft effective alternatives.

Consider, for example, the occupation of Iraq—the highly flawed jewel in the crown of the Bush administration. From the perspective of progressive framing, what we immediately see is that the current situation Iraq is a betrayal of the core American principle of "We the People." The invasion and occupation did not include the people, but instead was sold to the public through strategic secrecy. The initial act of concealment was a false connection between the perpetrators of the September 11, 2001, attacks (e.g., Al Qaeda) and the leadership of Iraq (e.g., Saddam Hussein). Not only were the facts underlying that connection known to be false, but more significantly, the means to discover their fraudulence were hidden from the people by a veil of intelligence classification. Even when requests for information were made that President Bush was required by law to answer, he advanced and maintained a policy that excluded the constitutional means of government afforded to the people. Having lead to a seemingly endless series of military mistakes, the Bush policy in Iraq first and foremost has engendered an overwhelming need to restore American principle to American policy—to displace "secrecy" with "responsibility," and to reconnect the people's policy to the people.

A progressive policy on Iraq, therefore, begins with the imperative to restore progressive principle to American government. And in fact, since oversight and accountability of the Executive Branch by Congress was restored in the wake of the 2006 midterm elections, it has became possible again to refocus the American Iraq policy on a long-term vision of progressive "smart" security.

The debate on America's collapsing healthcare system is similarly frustrated not by lack of good ideas, but by the absence of a progressive frame. The problem with healthcare might seem at first simply to be the high cost of insurance, but in fact it is a much broader crisis of the core American principle of opportunity. The idea that America is a place of opportunity has become clouded by financial doomsday scenarios that trap the American public in a political horror film about the uncontrollable "cost" of caring for its citizens. In this problematic frame, the monetary "price" of healthcare has become the primary focus of discussion, and, as a result, many Americans now routinely accept that good healthcare is just too expensive or that for a business to invest in the health of its employees will lead to the loss of jobs. These conclusions are not only wrong, they are dangerous. But as long as we accept this financial frame for the debate on healthcare, we will continue to be trapped in these losing scenarios.

A progressive policy on universal healthcare, therefore, cannot merely respond to fears about affordability, but must reframe the debate with the initial promise to restore the American principle of opportunity. Just as Franklin D. Roosevelt restored hope to America with a "New Deal" of economic achievements, progressives must restore opportunity to American with a "New Deal" for healthcare, such as:

- Investment in new community clinics and local hospitals
- Renewed health education and physical fitness in schools
- New approaches to physician and registered nurse training
- Nutritional regulation of the entire fast-food industry
- Increase in the minimum wage

Progressive ideas about health and healthcare do not ignore economics, they simply frame economics in terms of opportunity rather than mere profit and loss. By framing healthcare in terms of a "restored promise of opportunity," discussions of new healthcare possibilities can flourish without being stomped out by the fear of costs.

No other progressive policy discussion is more in need of reframing than the question of fair elections. While the problem with fair elections is often discussed in terms of "electronic" versus "paper" balloting systems, the debate is in fact about a much larger collapse in the most fundamental of all American principles: faith.

Over the past decade, conservatives have reframed the idea of "faith" in narrow terms having to do with specific forms of spiritual belief and religious dogma. Individuals can and should always be free to decide for themselves the meaning of spirituality. The more important principles, however, that have been lost in the narrow religious frame has been "faith" in the guarantee of free fair elections, "faith" in our system of governance, and "faith" in the Constitution. The massive voter fraud scandals of the 2000 and 2004 presidential elections, coupled with the rise of a vast network of corporate influence in Washington, D.C. has shaken the faith Americans once held in our electoral and representative system. It was not until the 2006 midterm elections that this faith began to be restored, although plenty of voting districts were still fraught with problems. From within this frame of lost "faith," it is no surprise that the introduction of so-called "eVote" computerized and paperless balloting systems is often met with such widespread skepticism.

A progressive policy on fair elections, therefore, should not begin by choosing an upper limit for individual campaign donations or the best machine for voting, but by promising to restore the public's "faith" in our constitutional process. One step towards restoring that faith would be to establish an annual Election Day holiday. In conjunction with this new Election Day holiday, progressives could work towards a series of fair election measures, such as:

- Public funding for campaigns
- Civics curriculum for schools
- National standardization for paper-receipt ballot systems
- Independent non-profit oversight board for elections

Without framing fair elections in terms of "faith," progressive efforts will fail before they begin. But once election reform is framed in terms of restoring faith in our constitutional system, real tangible solutions can move forward with great speed.

The 3 C's of Conservative Control

Participation, principle, promise—progressive framing is not just a marketing trick to repackage old ideas to make them more palatable, but an ongoing process that transforms the habits and experience of American democracy. However, once the debate has been reframed and a progressive vision begins to shape the American landscape, how then do we frame the opposite of progressivism? What is conservatism from the perspective of a progressive frame?

Interestingly, when approached from a progressive frame, the question of what constitutes a conservative vision is not "military strength," "fiscal conservatism" or "family values," but political behavior relative to our three core American principles:

- We the people
- Opportunity for all
- Faith in the Constitution

Over the course of his nearly two terms in office, President Bush has attempted to dismantle the primacy of "We the People" through his ongoing quest for unchecked executive control of government. Bush's "top down" approach to governing has entailed using legal trickery to circumvent Congressional oversight, most notably through his unprecedented abuse of the presidential signing statement as a strategy for claiming exemption from specific U.S. laws.[8] In fact, Bush was not the first conservative President to aspire to total control over the Federal government, even if he was the most relentless in his efforts to achieve it. The country witnessed in President Nixon's actions, for example, a similar aspiration for unfettered executive power.

American belief in "opportunity for all" has been similarly undercut by the spread of the conservative vision of the past few decades. The "trickle down" economics of President Reagan and the tax cut fixation of President George W. Bush, for example, both undermined the debate on equal opportunity for all in favor of a debate that emphasized capital gains and capital preservation. From a progressive frame, conservatives have fixated for decades on dismantling programs designed to help the poor, deregulating markets that protect small investors, and undermining labor laws that protect hourly workers. The result has been a series of conservative measures that has suffocated "opportunity for all" while breathing new life into a "wealth rules" culture in America—the type of power that has not held such prominence since Theodore Roosevelt confronted the powerful robber barons of America's so-called "Gilded Age."[9]

This conservatism, in other words, bears a striking resemblance to the worldview of an unethical businessman—autocratic, greedy, and arrogant.

Unfortunately, this corporatism is only part of the picture. The second, equally troubling aspect of this conservatism when viewed from within a progressive frame is its resemblance to radical clericalism. The past ten years has witnessed a rise in American religious extremism, which has as its goal to give primacy to the dictates of specific religious dogma over the principles of the Constitution itself.

Of equal concern from the perspective of a progressive worldview, conservatism has also advanced an imperial policy vis-à-vis other nations, advocating military conquest to expand American dominance in the world. By advancing this imperialist worldview, conservatism has trapped the American military—and the future of America along with it—in a failed and impossible policy of conquering and refashioning an entire part of the world.

Corporatism, clericalism and conquest. A progressive vision reveals each of these three attributes of contemporary "conservatism" as not only foreign to American principle as understood throughout our history, but actually corrosive to the foundation of the American constitutional system itself. And that is perhaps the most damaging thing of all—how, from a progressive frame, conservatives have weakened America's faith in the Constitution by turning it into a document that excludes too many from the full participation, principals, and promise of citizenship.

Transformation

The personal and collective transformation that allows progressives to see and articulate their core attributes, as well as those of conservatism, extends far beyond the repackaging of ideas or the rephrasing of slogans. Progressives are neither "new" Democrats nor "old" Democrats, neither the antithesis of Republicans nor the inheritors of liberalism. Progressivism is rooted in America's constitutional era and continues to emerge in our culture today.

But lasting political transformation does not advance without people to drive it forward. When we make the choice to frame the debate, that transformation begins, each morning, each moment, every day. It happens in speeches, phone calls, letters, and conversations. Transformation happens as we read, as we write, as we speak, and as we listen. By framing the debate, we take on the challenge of transforming American political culture, and in so doing we also take up the habits, principles, and vision that root us all together in the American tradition, and carry it towards the future.

SELECTED REFERENCES

Andrews, John A. *Lyndon Johnson and the Great Society*. Chicago: Ivan R. Dee, 1998.

Armstrong, Jerome and Markos Moulitsas Zúniga. *Crashing the Gates: Netroots, Grassroots, and the Rise of People-Powered Politics*. White River Junction, VT: Chelsea Green Publishing Company, 2006.

Bateson, Gregory. *Steps to an Ecology of Mind: Collected Essays in Anthropology, Psychiatry, Evolution, and Epistemology*. Chicago: University Of Chicago Press, 1972.

Brands, H. W. *Woodrow Wilson 1913-1921*. New York: Times Books, 2003.

Bunyan, John. *The Pilgrim's Progress*. New York: Oxford University Press, 2003 (1678).

Foote, Shelby. *The Civil War, A Narrative: Fredericksburg to Meridian*. New York: Random House, 1958.

Frank, Thomas. *What's The Matter With Kansas: How Conservatives Won the Heart of America*. New York: Henry Holt, 2004.

Frost, Robert. *The Poetry of Robert Frost: The Collected Poems, Complete and Unabridged*. Edited by Edward Connery Lathem. New York: Henry Holt, 1969.

Gable, John A. *The Bullmoose Years: Theodore Roosevelt and the Progressive Party*. Port Washington, NY: Kennikat Press, 1978.

Gilmore, Dan. *We The Media: Grassroots Journalism by the People for the People*. New York: O'Reilly Media, 2004.

Goffman, Erving. *Frame Analysis: An Essay on the Organization of Experience*. New York: Harper & Row, 1974.

Greenwald, Glenn. *How Would A Patriot Act: Defending American Values from a President Run Amok*. San Francisco: Working Assets Publishing, 2006.

Grinder, John and Richard Bandler. *Reframing: Neurolinguistic Programming and the Transformation of Meaning.* Moab, UT: Real People Press, 1983.

Johnson, Chalmers A. *The Sorrows of Empire: Militarism, Secrecy and the End of the Republic.* New York: Metropolitan Books, 2004.

King, Jr., Martin Luther. *A Call to Conscience: The Landmark Speeches of Dr. Martin Luther King, Jr.* Edited by Clayborne Carson and Kris Shepard. New York: IPM/Warner Books, 2001.

Kittay, Eva Feder. *Metaphor: It's Cognitive Force and Linguistic Structure.* New York: Oxford University Press, 1987.

LaFeber, Walter. *America, Russia, and the Cold War, 1945-1980,* 7th edition. New York: McGraw-Hill,1993.

Lakoff, George and Mark Johnson. *Metaphors We Live By.* Chicago: University of Chicago Press, 1980.

Lakoff, George. *Don't Think of an Elephant! Know Your Values and Frame the Debate.* White River Junction, VT: Chelsea Green Publishing Company, 2004.

Lakoff, George. *Moral Politics: How Liberals and Conservatives Think.* Chicago: University of Chicago Press, 1996.

Lakoff, George. *Thinking Points: Communicating Our American Values and Vision.* New York: Farrar, Straus and Giroux, 2006.

Markowitz, Norman D. *The Rise and Fall of the People's Century: Henry A. Wallace and American Liberalism, 1941-1948.* New York: The Free Press, 1973.

Meyer, Susan E. *James Montgomery Flagg.* New York: Watson-Guptill, 1974.

Roosevelt, Theodore. *Letters and Speeches.* edited by Louis Auchincloss. New York: Library of America, 2004.

Smith, Marc A. and Peter Kollock, eds. *Communities in Cyberspace.* New York: Routledge, 1999.

Stone, Douglas, Bruce Patton and Sheila Heen. *Difficult Conversations: How to Discuss What Matters Most.* New York: Penguin Books, 1999.

Unger, Nancy C. *Fighting Bob la Follette: The Righteous Reformer.* Chapel Hill, NC: University of North Carolina Press, 2000.

Williams, Raymond. *Keywords: A Vocabulary of Culture and Society.* New York: Oxford University Press, 1976.

NOTES

PREFACE

1. Raymond Williams, *Keywords: A Vocabulary of Culture and Society* (New York: Oxford University Press, 1976), 244.

2. For more on the history of progressive movements in America, see John A. Gable, *The Bullmoose Years: Theodore Roosevelt and the Progressive Party* (Port Washington, NY: Kennikat Press, 1978); Nancy C. Unger, *Fighting Bob la Follette: The Righteous Reformer*, (Chapel Hill, NC: University of North Carolina Press, 2000); Norman D. Markowitz, *The Rise and Fall of the People's Century: Henry A. Wallace and American liberalism, 1941-1948*, (New York: The Free Press, 1973).

1. FRAMERS AND FRAMING

1. *The American Heritage Dictionary of the English Language, Fourth Edition*, (New York: Hougton Mifflin, 2006).

2. Gregory Bateson, S*teps to an Ecology of Mind: Collected Essays in Anthropology, Psychiatry, Evolution, and Epistemology* (Chicago: University Of Chicago Press, 1972).

3. Erving Goffman, *Frame Analysis: An Essay on the Organization of Experience* (New York: Harper & Row, 1974).

4. John Grinder and Richard Bandler, *Reframing: Neurolinguistic Programming and the Transformation of Meaning* (Moab, UT: Real People Press, 1983).

5. Douglas Stone, Bruce Patton and Sheila Heen, *Difficult Conversations: How to Discuss What Matters Most* (New York: Penguin Books, 1999).

6. George Lakoff, *Don't Think of an Elephant! Know Your Values and Frame the Debate* (White River Junction, VT: Chelsea Green Publishing Company, 2004).

7. Ibid, xv.

8. George Lakoff, *Moral Politics: How Liberals and Conservatives Think* (Chicago: University of Chicago Press, 1996).

9. To read all public statements by the President, see http://www.white house.gov/news

10. Jeffrey Feldman, "Mission Statement," *Frameshop*, January 2005, http://jeffrey-feldman.typepad.com/frameshop/2005/01/frameshop_will_.html

11. For a full discussion of the logical construction of metaphors, see George Lakoff and Mark Johnson, *Metaphors We Live By* (Chicago: University of Chicago Press, 1980); Eva Feder Kittay, *Metaphor: It's Cognitive Force and Linguistic Structure* (New York: Oxford University Press, 1987).

12. Jeffrey Feldman, "Personal Retirement Accounts (PRA's)," *Frameshop*, January 2, 2005, http://jeffrey-feldman.typepad.com/frameshop/2005/01/frame shop_perso.html

13. Dan Gilmore, *We The Media: Grassroots Journalism by the People for the People*, (New York: O'Reilly Media, 2004).

2. VOICE OF THE COUNTRY

1. The texts of presidential speeches are available from a variety of books and websites. For a full text of this speech, see "First Inaugural Address," *George Washington Speeches*, The Miller Center of Public Affairs: Presidential Speech Collection, http://millercenter.virginia.edu/scripps/diglibrary/prezspeeches/washing ton/gw_1789_0430.html

3. WISE AND FRUGAL

1. For a full text of this speech, see "First Inaugural Address," *Thomas Jefferson Speeches*, The Miller Center of Public Affairs: Presidential Speech Collection, http://millercenter.virginia.edu/scripps/diglibrary/prezspeeches/jefferson/tj_1801_0304.html

2. "Burthened" is a late 18th-Century spelling of "burdened."

3. Jefferson, "First Inaugural Address," ibid.

4. Al Gore, "American Heresy," (speech, Hyatt Regency, Washington, DC, April 27, 2005). Salon.com, http://dir.salon.com/story/opinion/feature/2005/04/27/al_gore/index.html

4. OF THE PEOPLE

1. For a full text of this speech, see "Gettysburg Address," *Abraham Lincoln Speeches*, The Miller Center of Public Affairs: Presidential Speech Collection, http://millercenter.virginia.edu/scripps/diglibrary/prezspeeches/lincoln/al_1863_1119.html

2. Shelby Foote, *The Civil War, A Narrative: Fredericksburg to Meridian* (New York: Random House, 1958).

5. THE MUCK RAKE

1. For a full text of this speech, see "Theodore Roosevelt: The Man with the Muck Rake," *Speech Archive, Program in Presidential Rhetoric presented by the Department of Communication at Texas A & M University*, http://comm.tamu.edu/pres/speeches/trmuck.html

2. John Bunyan, *The Pilgrim's Progress*, (New York: Oxford University Press, 2003).

3. Carl Cameron, "Lieberman Accuses Lamont Camp of Hacking Web Site, *Fox News*, August 8, 2006, http://www.foxnews.com/story/0,2933,207401,00.html

4. David Sirota, "Lieberman Campaign Blames Its Incompetence on Lamont," *The Huffington Post*, August 8 2006, http://www.huffingtonpost.com/david-sirota/lieberman-campaign-blames_b_26813.html

6. HIGHWAYS OF THE WORLD

1. For a full text of this speech, see "President Woodrow Wilson's War Message," *World War I Document Archive*, http://www.lib.byu.edu/~rdh/wwi/1917/wilswarm.html

2. Ibid.

3. H. W. Brands, *Woodrow Wilson 1913-1921* (New York: Times Books, 2003).

4. Wilson, "War Message," ibid.

5. Ibid.

6. Ibid.

7. HAPPINESS IS ACHIEVEMENT

1. For a full text and audio recording of this speech, see "First Inaugural Address," *Franklin D. Roosevelt Speeches, The Miller Center of Public Affairs, Presidential Speech Collection*, http://millercenter.virginia.edu/scripps/diglibrary/prezspeeches/roosevelt/fdr_1933_0304.html

2. See "Address to Congress Requesting a Declaration of War," *Franklin D. Roosevelt Speeches*, The Miller Center of Public Affairs: Presidential Speech Collection, http://millercenter.virginia.edu/scripps/diglibrary/prezspeeches/roosevelt/fdr_1941_1208.html

3. F. Roosevelt, "First Inaugural Address," ibid.

4. Ibid.

5. Susan E. Meyer, *James Montgomery Flagg* (New York: Watson-Guptill, 1974).

8. US AGAINST THEM

1. For a full text and audio recording of this speech, see "Inaugural Address," *Harry S. Truman Speeches*, The Miller Center of Public Affairs: Presidential Speech Collection, http://millercenter.virginia.edu/scripps/diglibrary/prezspeeches/tru man/hst_1949_0120.html

2. Walter Lafeber, *America, Russia, and the Cold War, 1945-1980*, 7th edition (New York: McGraw-Hill, 1993).

3. Bush began to push this "us" against "them" formula in the days leading up to his address to the United Nations (November 10, 2001). In a press conference with French President Jacques Chirac, for example, Bush said, "You are either with us or you are against us in the fight against terror," orienting the national debate strongly in the logic of the "enemy" frame. See "President Welcomes President Chirac to the White House," White House Website, November 6, 2001, http://www.whitehouse.gov/news/releases/2001/11/20011106-4.html

4. Truman, "Inaugural Address," ibid.

5. Ibid.

6. "President Delivers State of the Union Address," White House Website, January 29, 2002, http://www.whitehouse.gov/news/releases/2002/01/20020129 - 11.html

7. See "Remarks by the President at the Missouri Victory 2006 Rally," White House Website, November 3, 2006, http://www.whitehouse.gov/news/releases/2006/11/20061103-2.html

9. BALANCE IN PROGRESS

1. For a full text and audio recording of this speech, see "Farewell Address," *Dwight D. Eisenhower Speeches*, The Miller Center of Public Affairs: Presidential Speech Collection, http://millercenter.virginia.edu/scripps/diglibrary/prezspeeches/eisenhower/dde_1961_0116.html

2. For an excellent discussion of the links between the build up of the military-industrial complex and the rise of American imperialism, see Chalmers A. Johnson, *The Sorrows of Empire: Militarism, Secrecy and the End of the Republic* (New York: Metropolitan Books, 2004).

3. Geov Parrish, "Making Sense of the Abramoff Scandal," *Alternet*, December 20, 2005, http://www.alternet.org/story/29827

4. "Private Warriors," *Frontline*, June 21, 2005, Produced by Martin Smith, *PBS*. Also posted in full at http://www.pbs.org/wgbh/pages/frontline/shows/warriors/view

5. David Espo, "Pelosi Said She Would Drain GOP Swamp," *Washington Post*, October 6, 2006, posted at http://www.washingtonpost.com/wpdyn/con tent/article/2006/10/06/AR2006100600056.html.

10. ASK AND ANSWER

1. For a full text and audio recording of this speech, see "Inaugural Address," *John F. Kennedy Speeches,* The Miller Center of Public Affairs: Presidential Speech Collection,http://millercenter.virginia.edu/scripps/diglibrary/prezspeeches/ken nedy/jfk_1961_0120.html

2. Ibid.

3. President Bush Meets With Senator Reid And Senator Durbin At The White House," White House Website, November 10, 2006, posted at: http://www.whitehouse.gov/news/releases/2006/11/20061110.html

4. Ibid.

5. "Where It Starts," Spitzer-Patterson 2006, Campaign ad, posted at http://www.spitzerpaterson.com.

6. Kennedy, "Inaugural Address," ibid.

7. "The Apollo Alliance provides a message of optimism and hope, framed around rejuvenating our nation's economy by creating the next generation of American industrial jobs and treating clean energy as an economic and security mandate to rebuild America. America needs to hope again, to dream again, to think big, and to be called to the best of our potential by tapping the optimism and can-do spirit that is embedded in our nation's history. In 1961, John F. Kennedy challenged the nation to send a man to the moon and return him safely home again within the decade. It was an audacious dare. . . . Now America has an Apollo project for the 21st century." See, "About Us," Apollo Alliance, http://www.apolloalliance.org/about_the_alliance.

11. BUILD A SOCIETY

1. For a full text and audio recording of this speech, see "Remarks at the University of Michigan," *Lyndon B. Johnson Speeches,* The Miller Center of Public Affairs, Presidential Speech Collection, http://millercenter.virginia.edu/scripps/di glibrary/prezspeeches/johnson/lbj_1964_0522.html

2. Ibid.

3. John A. Andrews, *Lyndon Johnson and the Great Society* (Chicago: Ivan R. Dee, 1998).

4. Lakoff, *Moral Politics*, 1996.

5. Johnson, "Remarks at the University of Michigan," ibid.

6. Ibid.

7. Glenn Kessler, "Clinton Gather's World Leaders, Non Partisan Conference Focuses on Global Improvement," *Washington Post*, September 16, 2005.

12. I HAVE SUCCEEDED

1. For a full text, audio and video recording of this speech, see "Richard Nixon: Resignation Speech," *American Rhetoric*, https://www.americanrhetoric.com/speeches/richardnixonresignationspeech.html

2. Progressives often talk about the difference between framing and spin by critiquing the work of Republican communications guru Frank Luntz. See George Lakoff and Sam Ferguson, "Framing Versus Spin: Rockridge as opposed to Luntz," *Buzzflash*, June 9, 2006, http://www.buzzflash.com/contribu tors/06/06/con06234.html

3. Nixon, "Resignation Speech," ibid.

4. Theodore Roosevelt, *Letters and Speeches*, ed. by Louis Auchincloss (New York: Library of America, 2004).

5. Jeffrey Feldman, "Frameshop: How 'Swiftboating' Works and What To Do About It," *Frameshop*, January 16, 2006, http://jeffrey-feldman.typepad.com/frameshop/2006/01/frameshop_how_s.html

6. Patrick Murphy for Congress, "They Swiftboated—And You Responded," *MyDD*, October 16, 2006, http://www.mydd.com/sto ry/2006/10/16/13138/452

7. For a discussion of "trolls" in sociological perspective, see Judith S. Donath, "Identity and Deception in the Virtual Community," in *Communities in Cyberspace*, ed. by Marc A. Smith and Peter Kollock (New York: Routledge, 1999).

8. For a debunking of the Mussolini train myth, see R.J.B. Bosworth, *Mussolini: The Biography* (London: Hodder Arnold, 2002).

9. Jeffrey Feldman, "Frameshop: The Knockout Punch," *Frameshop*, January 10, 2005, http://jeffrey-feldman.typepad.com/frameshop/2005/01/frame shop_the_k.html

13. DOWN THAT PATH

1. For a full text and audio recording of this speech, see "Crisis of Confidence Speech," *Jimmy Carter Speeches*, The Miller Center of Public Affairs: Presidential Speech Collection, http://millercenter.virginia.edu/scripps/diglib rary/prezspeeches/carter/jec_1979_0715.html

2. Lakoff and Johnson, *Metaphors We Live By*, 14-21.

3. Carter, "Crisis of Confidence Speech," ibid.

4. Ibid.

5. *The Poetry of Robert Frost: The Collected Poems, Complete and Unabridged*, ed. by Edward Connery Lathem (New York: Henry Holt, 1969).

6. Carter, "Crisis of Confidence Speech," ibid.

7. Lakoff and Johnson, *Metaphors We Live By*, 22-24.

14. A SMALL STORY

1. For a full text and audio recording of this speech, see "Farewell Address," *Ronald Reagan Speeches, The Miller Center of Public Affairs, Presidential Speech Collection*, http://millercenter.virginia.edu/scripps/diglibrary/prezspeeches/rea gan/rwr_1989_0111.html

2. Ibid.

3. "Text: Senator John Edwards Speech To DNC," *Washington Post*, July 28, 2004, posted at http://www.washingtonpost.com/wp-dyn/articles/A22230-2004Jul28.html

4. Richard W. Stevenson, "Of The Many Deaths In Iraq, One Mother's Loss Becomes A Problem For The President," *New York Times*, August 8, 2005, http://www.nytimes.com/2005/08/08/politics/08crawford.html; Jeffrey Feldman, "Frameshop The 'Grieving Mom' Frame," *Frameshop*, August 14, 2005, http://jeffrey-feldman.typepad.com/frameshop/2005/08/frameshop_the_g.html

5. Jeffrey Feldman, "Frameshop: The Face of Protest is a Changin'," *Frameshop*, March 21, 2005, http://jeffrey-feldman.typepad.com/frameshop/2005/03/the_ face_of_pro.html

6. Tim Craig and Michael D. Shear, "Allen Quip Provokes Outrage, Apology," *Washington Post*, August 15, 2006.

15. GOVERNMENT IS A PERSON

1. For a full text and audio recording of this speech, see "Second Inaugural Address," *William J. Clinton Speeches*, The Miller Center of Public Affairs: Presidential Speech Collection, http://millercenter.virginia.edu/scripps/diglibrary/prezspeeches/clinton/wjc_1997_0120.html

2. Clinton, "Second Inaugural Address," ibid.

3. Ibid.

4. Ibid.

5. Martin Luther King Jr., "I See The Promised Land," April 3, 1968, in *A Call to Conscience: The Landmark Speeches of Dr. Martin Luther King, Jr.,* ed. Clayborne Carson and Kris Shepard (New York: IPM/Warner Books, 2001).

6. Clinton, "Second Inaugural Address," ibid.

7. *The American Prospect*, posted this "elevator pitch" as part of a call to define liberalism in 30 words or less. See, "The Liberal Agenda by the Readers

of The American Prospect," January 2005, http://www.prospect.org/web/page.
ww?section=root&name=Liberal+Agenda

8. Jason Patent and George Lakoff, "Conceptual Levels: Bringing It Home To Values," *Rockridge Institute*, http://www.rockridgeinstitute.org/projects/stra tegic/conceptlevels.

9. For a list and discussion of progressive values, see George Lakoff, *Thinking Points: Communicating Our American Values and Vision* (New York: Farrar, Straus and Giroux, 2006).

10. Hillary Rodham Clinton, *It Takes A Village* (New York: Touchstone, 1996).

11. Clinton, "Second Inaugural Address," ibid.

12. For a copy of this speech, see Carson and Shepard, *A Call to Conscience: The Landmark Speeches of Dr. Martin Luther King, Jr.*. Also posted at http://www. stanford.edu/group/King/publications/speeches/address_at_march_on_washington.pdf

16. EVIL WILL ATTACK

1. For a full text, audio and video recording of this speech, see "State of the Union Address," White House Website, January 29, 2002, http://www.white house.gov/news/releases/2002/01/20020129-11.html

2. For a good description of Luntz, see "The Persuaders," *Frontline*, June 21, 2005. Directed by Barak Goodman and Rachel Dretzin, produced by Rachel Dretzin, Barak Goodman, Muriel Soenens, *PBS*. Transcript posted in full at http://www.pbs.org/wgbh/pages/frontline/shows/persuaders/etc/script.html

3. Bush, "State of the Union Address," ibid.

4. Ibid.

5. *Human Rights Watch*, "Q & A: Military Commissions Act of 2006," posted at http://hrw.org/backgrounder/usa/qna1006; Charles Babington and Jonathan Weisman, "Senate Approves Detainee Bill Backed by Bush," *Washington Post*, September 29, 2006; Keith Olbermann, "Special Comment: Beginning of the End of American, " *Countdown*, October 19, 2006, http://www.msnbc.msn. com/id/15321167/; For a great discussion of the connection between President Bush's politics and his attempts to undermine the Constitution, see Glenn Greenwald, *How Would A Patriot Act: Defending American Values from a President Run Amok* (San Francisco: Working Assets Publishing, 2006).

6. "Press Conference of the President," White House Website, September 16, 2006, posted at: http://www.whitehouse.gov/news/releases/2006/09/20060915 -2.html.

7. Jeffrey Feldman, "Frameshop: The Ticking Bomb Frame," *Frameshop*,

November 9, 2005, http://jeffrey-feldman.typepad.com/frameshop/2005/11/frameshop_the_t.html

8. The Republican National Committee's controversial 2006 political advertisement "Stakes" was posted for viewing during the election campaign on the Republican National Committee website, http://www.gop.com/Multimedia.

17. THE THREE P'S OF PROGRESSIVE POLITICS

1. Lincoln, "Gettysburg Address," ibid.

2. Carter, "Crisis of Confidence," ibid.

3. T. Roosevelt, "Address on the Cornerstone Laying for the Cannon Building," ibid; Johnson, "University of Michigan Commencement Address," ibid.

4. Wilson, "War Message," ibid; Truman, "Inaugural Address," ibid.

5. Eisenhower, "Farewell Message," ibid.

6. Kennedy, "Inaugural Address," ibid; Clinton, "Second Inaugural," ibid.

7. F. Roosevelt, "First Inaugural," ibid

8. Greenwald, *How Would A Patriot Act*, ibid.

9. For a discussion about the emergence of a new Robber Baron Era, see Thom Hartmann, *Screwed: The Undeclared War against the Middle Class—And What We Can Do About It* (San Francisco: Berrett-Koehler Publishers, Inc., 2006).